W9-BSV-186

How to Be an
Open-minded
Christian
without Losing Your
Faith

How to Be an
Open-minded
Christian
without Losing Your
Faith

JAN G. LINN

CHALICE
PRESS

© Copyright 2002 by Jan G. Linn

All rights reserved. No part of this book may be reproduced without written permission from Chalice Press, P.O. Box 179, St. Louis, MO 63166-0179.

Bible quotations, unless otherwise noted, are from the *New Revised Standard Version Bible*, copyright 1989, Division of Christian Education of the National Council of Churches of Christ in the United States of America. Used by permission. All rights reserved.

Cover design: Michael Domínguez
Cover art: Detail from banner by Joseph McNally, Singapore, from IMAGE, published by Asian Christian Art Association, vol. 64, 1995
Interior design: Hui-Chu Wang
Art direction: Michael Domínguez

This book is printed on acid-free, recycled paper.

Visit Chalice Press on the World Wide Web at
www.chalicepress.com

10 9 8 7 6 5 4 3 2 1   02 03 04 05 06

Library of Congress Cataloging–in–Publication Data

Linn, Jan.
   How to be an open-minded Christian without losing your faith /
Jan G. Linn.
        p.   cm.
   ISBN 0-8272-1443-X (alk. paper)
   1. Theology, Doctrinal—Popular works.   I. Title.
   BT77 .L53   2001
   230—dc21   2001006036

Printed in the United States of America

The great middle ground is that which maintains both the objectivity of truth and [the human] incapacity, either individually or collectively, to attain it.

— D. Elton Trueblood
Philosophy of Religion

Contents

The Bible is the gift of God for the people of God.
Authority is an inside job.
Inspiration is the breath of God then and now.

Jesus was a man.
Jesus is more than a man.
Jesus was a teaching prophet, not a prophetic teacher.
There is nothing original about sin.
Jesus' crucifixion was more than the death of a good man.
The resurrection is more than an empty tomb.
The resurrection is also more than having faith.
Salvation is a gift of God.
Judgment is better than we think.
Forgiveness is at the same time awful and wonderful.
Heaven and hell are more than places to go.
Miracles are a sign of God's future in the present.
Communion is not just a supper.
Helping the poor is more than lending a helping hand.

God really is.
God really is personal.
God is not gender-neutral.

God is "here and "there."
God is free to do whatever God chooses to do.
God is not a soft touch.

The Holy Spirit is a lot more than a holy ghost.
The Holy Spirit makes baptism something more than getting wet.
The Holy Spirit's presence or power plays no favorites.
We get the Holy Spirit's power the old-fashioned way.

Tough issues put Christian maturity to the test.
None of us is God.
Knowing what's right is sometimes as clear as mud.
Premarital sex is about more than yes or no.
Divorce is worse than you may think.
Homosexuality is about more than sex.
Abortion is about more than being pro-life or pro-choice.
There is more to capital punishment than meets the eye.
Church and state need protection from each other.

Lukewarm faith is not limited to an ancient city in Asia Minor.
A little knowledge can go a long way.
Fear is no match for divine love.
Open-minded also means open-hearted.

Acknowledgments

How a book comes to be written is always a story in itself that says as much about context as it does about author or subject. This book arose within a faith community that is part of a Protestant denomination that has a long tradition of living with the creative tensions born of freethinking people coming together. In this respect our communion is quite reflective of American culture, a fact of life that has itself produced more than a few points of tension in our two-hundred year history. In every respect I am the child of both my faith community and my larger culture. Working, therefore, to find a reliable faith foundation on which to base one's life amid the changing tides of diverse religious and cultural heritages has almost become second nature to me. In a manner of speaking, I have gotten the faith I have the old-fashioned way. I've "earned it," the result of hard work and more than a little wrestling with God.

The marvelous thing is that I have been nurtured all the way by this denomination of mine, more than a few times by simply being permitted to wander as far as my mind and heart would carry me until I found my way. For this I am grateful beyond words. Whatever strengths this book brings to the topics under discussion have in no small way been made possible by this amazing company of Christians. Within it, and also beyond it in the larger faith and interfaith communities of God's people, have been so many examples of faith and reason by which I have been blessed. In particular I want to thank a colleague and friend of long ago, Rabbi Morris Shapiro, and the congregants of Agudath Shalom Temple, whose model of faith and faithfulness first gave birth to the impulse that has burned in me all these years to learn how to be an open-minded Christian. My gratitude also goes to Albert Pennybacker, who read portions of the material, but more importantly lives the kind of faith to which this book seeks to be a witness. Appreciation also goes to a group of clergy colleagues who gave helpful suggestions in the earliest stages of the chapters on Jesus. To Joyce Digby I am greatly in debt for her amazing critical eye that made this book read far better than it would have without her help. And to my wife, Joy, who endured with grace and understanding the hours spent writing that added to her work in this immense ministry we share of starting a new church. Besides that, she is always ready to read the drafts of books I am writing, and in the process she manages with uncanny ability to differentiate the moments better served by kindness than candor. It is a role fraught with the risks of being the bearer of unwanted news, but one she fills with exceptional grace and balance.

Finally, my association with Chalice Press, spanning more than a few years and books now, is one I value more than words can adequately express. But it is never out of season to say thank you. So to all who work there to make books like this possible, "Thank you!"

Jan G. Linn
Apple Valley
The First Day of Fall, 2001

Introduction

In the 1925 trial in Dayton, Tennessee, sometimes called "the monkey trial," Clarence Darrow served as attorney for defendant John Scopes, who was charged with violating the state law prohibiting the teaching of evolution in public schools. Darrow made the unorthodox decision to call the state's attorney, William Jennings Bryan, to the stand. Bryan readily agreed, and the exchange between the two was extraordinary. At one point Darrow asked his star witness the approximate date he believed the Great Flood occurred. Bryan hesitated. Some Christians were claiming it was 2400 B.C.E. Darrow asked Bryan if he knew how that date had been arrived at.

"I never made a calculation," Bryan responded.

"A calculation from what?" Darrow asked.

"I could not say."

"From the generations of man?"

"I would not want to say," answered Bryan.

"What do you think?" Darrow then asked.

"I do not think about things I don't think about," Bryan responded.

"Do you think about things you do think about?" asked Darrow.

"Well, sometimes..." Bryan answered as laughter broke out in the courtroom.[1]

This book has been written for Christians who want to think about things that they think about, but who do not necessarily think about them in the same way as many whose views—both conservative and liberal—represent what they consider to be theological extremes. It is also for Christian seekers who want to know what they can believe without coming across as either condemning of non-Christians or wishy-washy about their own faith. Essentially, then, this book is for all Christians and would-be

1

Christians who want a faith that is grounded in biblical teaching and church tradition yet open-minded in the search for truth.

In today's environment voices that do not adequately represent the beliefs and attitudes of moderate Christians are often the loudest. On one end of the theological spectrum are those who speak about matters of faith and morals in absolute terms. For them the Bible is God's Word, and they know what that is. All anyone has to do to get an answer for any vexing question is to accept what these protectors of the faith say that the Bible says. It's as easy as that. This, for example, is how the Southern Baptist Convention justified its rejection of women clergy as senior pastors. As the Reverend Adrian Rogers, who chaired the drafting committee on the adopted resolution, stated, "This is what God says."[2]

The opposite end of the spectrum is represented by scholars such as those in the Jesus Seminar, a group whose purpose is to identify the real Jesus as they sift through the New Testament to distinguish what he actually said from what was attributed to him. It is not a new thing they are doing. The search for the historical Jesus has a long history in scholarly circles. But to date it would appear that, with a few exceptions,[3] the fruit of the group's labors is to debunk the naive belief that the man Jesus actually said much of anything the New Testament attributes to him.[4]

There is a wholly independent partner in this approach to scripture, theorists variously labeled as "minimalists" or "revisionists" who have reached similar conclusions about the Old Testament. Their assessment is that the Israel of the Bible and the Israel of history bear little connection with each other, the former being the creation of Jewish writers during the Persian period in the sixth century and the latter being the "real" Israel they have discovered.[5]

This book seeks to offer an alternative to these views, articulating a perspective whose goal is to help ordinary Christians make sense of the faith they have without undermining it. It seeks also to help those who are not sure what to make of the Christian gospel to see that it does make sense. This perspective rejects the argument that faith and history are incompatible sources of knowledge or truth. We are attempting to identify those core beliefs that give Christians identity, a place to stand, so to speak, that allows them to witness to all the truth they know without claiming to know all the truth there is not only about matters of faith but also in regard to some of the most controversial issues of our day. In short, this book is for Christians and would-be Christians who have no desire to be judgmental toward others but who do want to be committed in their discipleship to Jesus.

In this new church ministry that I share with my wife, we encounter many unchurched young adults who are new to faith or are searching for a mature faith that is both biblical and flexible. They look to us for guidance and often ask the question, Just what kind of church are you? In many respects this book is an extended discussion of the answer we give them. Ministry is an appropriate context for this kind of endeavor. Abstract theologizing among professional scholars is an unfortunate modern development. As British theologian N. T. Wright has noted,

> The early creeds and the baptismal confessions which partly underlay them, were not little pieces of abstract theologizing to satisfy the curious intellect, but symbols which functioned as such, badges which marked out this community from others in terms of the god in whom they believed. From the start, Christian creeds were not so much a matter of "faith seeking understanding" as "community seeking definition"—and finding it in that which was believed about the true god...
>
> Christian "theology," then, was born and nurtured in the context of faith, worship, baptism and eucharist, and came to expression through the need to mark out the community which worshipped this god from communities that worshipped others.[6]

During the process of writing this material I decided to use it as a basis for a series of sermons that I preached over a three-month period. In addition there were two weekly opportunities for open discussion on the topics addressed. Not only did the congregation not tire from the series, they also offered challenging comments that helped me to see areas that needed greater clarity or rethinking altogether. It is a gift of grace to be in such a community of Christians who genuinely try to balance faith with open-mindedness and who have a strong desire to account for the hope that is within them, and to do it with gentleness and reverence (1 Pet. 3:15–16). This book is offered with the prayer that it will serve to encourage all Christians who share the same attitude.

1

What You Can Believe about the Bible

You may wonder why we would start with the Bible rather than God or Jesus. One reason is the fact that the Bible is a subject of such intense controversy among Christians. It is also the main source for the Christian story today. But the primary reason for making the Bible the beginning point is the fact that how we read it determines most of everything else we believe, as will become evident throughout the book. Thus, the Bible seems to be the best possible point of entry into these important matters of faith and morals. No prior knowledge of scripture and its development or of church tradition is presupposed as we begin. For the purpose of clarity the material is divided into subsections, but each should be understood within the context of the discussion as a whole.

The Bible is the gift of God for the people of God.

In some traditions clergy lift the bread and the wine of communion and invite the congregation to participate with the words, "The gifts of God for the people of God." The same thing can be said about the Bible. It is the gift of God for the people of

God. Though we would not call it a sacrament—that which conveys divine grace—hearing the Bible read and proclaimed can certainly be a sacramental moment wherein the people of God experience afresh the Spirit and power of God's presence.

A church without the Bible seems almost inconceivable, yet that is essentially what existed for at least the first three centuries of Christian history. It was not until sometime in the fourth century that the Christian Bible as we know it began to emerge with "canonical" status in the life of the church.[1] Among other things, this means that Christianity was not founded on the Bible. It was born in and grew from the personal testimonies of those who experienced the living presence of the crucified and raised Jesus. It was much later that the Bible became the force and resource it is in the Christian community today. This fact—that Christianity was not founded on the Bible—does not diminish the role of scripture as a guide to faith and even a means to experiencing the presence of the living Jesus. But it does highlight the potential for misunderstanding the role it has and should play as a guide and witness.

Every Christian knows that there are many ways of reading the Bible, as the many controversies surrounding these differences make painfully obvious. The lines separating Christians over the Bible are drawn in numerous directions between and within churches and denominations, but among these divisions two types of readings seem to occupy center stage—liberal and fundamentalist. In the search for an approach to reading the Bible that speaks to open-minded Christians, we need to make some general comments about these two polarities within which most Christians find themselves.

A liberal reading of the Bible is rooted in what is called *higher criticism*. This perspective draws on the tools of historical research common to other disciplines of study in understanding the Bible. Information gleaned from textual differences, the layers of development in the biblical material, the various sources of whole books and distinct sections, cultural analysis, historical background, and even extrabiblical material are all considered essential in understanding the biblical message. This approach sets no limits within which one must work to engage scripture. Interpretative boundaries are determined primarily by the extent to which one's view is taken seriously by the community of scholars. In short, from this perspective, the search for truth is wide open.

A fundamentalist reading of the Bible could not be more different. It sets boundaries beyond which no interpreter should go. It reads the Bible as the *literal* word of God, essentially meaning that God dictated the Bible. Thus, it is without error, or "infallible." Those who read the Bible in this way speak easily and often of "God's Word" speaking for itself and needing no human interpretation. All one must do to understand it is to accept the text as it stands. Naturally, then, questions raised by higher criticism are ignored or considered secondary in understanding the Bible.

As is sometimes the case, differences can make for strange bedfellows. In its own way each of these positions tends to lock the biblical message in the past. Higher critical study generally limits its task to discovering what texts meant at the time of Jesus and/or the first-century church. What they mean today is for others to decide. Fundamentalist interpreters, on the other hand, do not hesitate to collapse what a biblical text originally meant into what they believe it means today as well.

I think a more balanced approach lies somewhere in between these perspectives, recognizing the intellectual necessity of higher critical study but also taking seriously fundamentalism's concern for biblical authority. It begins with accepting the Bible as a sacred text written by human beings in all their limitations, and affirms that it contains the story of God's saving claim on humankind revealed in Israel and in Jesus, a claim that is universal and eternal. From this point of view the Bible is a book born of the inspiration of God's Spirit on the thoughts and words of the mortals who wrote it. Moreover, the Spirit of God at work when the Bible was written continues to work in the hearing and understanding of it in every generation. This way of reading scripture, therefore, affirms that the Bible *contains* the word of God without claiming it *is* the word of God. The words are not more than those of ordinary human beings, but the truth of its story is. That is what makes the Bible the gift of God for the people of God. God has spoken in and through these very human elements.

This open-minded approach to the Bible is actually an appeal to a historic concern for balancing faith and reason rather than ignoring the former (higher criticism) or being fearful of the latter (fundamentalism). This balance, which the church has desired but found difficult to maintain, is needed today more than ever. The key is to see faith and knowledge as partners in truth seeking, something neither liberalism nor fundamentalism does very well. Instead, both view knowledge as objective data one either accepts or rejects, the only difference between the groups being whose data is believed.[2] But knowledge is so much more than data, if for no other reason than because human perception is always a matter of seeing "in a mirror, dimly" (1 Cor. 13:12). Drawing from the insights of British theologian N. T. Wright,[3] let me illustrate what this means in terms of how we read the Bible.

Imagine yourself sitting at the breakfast table reading a newspaper article about a congressional debate on what to do to ensure the future of Social Security. One view of the information you are receiving is that there is a straight line from the event that took place and your knowledge of it via the newspaper report. Thus, a report of the event leads to your knowing what happened. But is this line straight after all? Consider these questions. Have you received knowledge of the debate itself or of the perception of the reporter who wrote the story about it? If all the participants in the debate have been sworn not to speak about it, can you be sure that even multiple reports about it provide you with "knowledge" of what took place? If, on the other hand, all participants are free to speak, are we hearing what in fact happened or their perceptions of it? Further, is your information of the event in fact "knowledge" of what actually happened or your perception of a story about what happened?

These and other questions like them point to a single reality. Knowledge is always the result of information's being filtered through human perception that is never perfect and can be quite skewed. This holds true whether it involves reading a newspaper story, doing scientific research, or reading the Bible. Wright defines this way of reading the Bible "critical realism." It is an acknowledgement that "worldviews...the lens through which the world is seen, the blueprint for how one should live in it, and above all the sense of identity and place which enables human beings to be what they are" are present in every reading of scripture.[4] Worldviews are the collective eye of a culture. A mind-set is the worldview of an individual; it shapes and influences the way a person assimilates and communicates information.[5] Moreover, the Bible itself has worldviews, according to Wright, because they are "the stuff of human experience."[6]

From this perspective reading the Bible is the engagement of both similar and differing worldviews and mind-sets in every respect: the writers and the reader and their cultural contexts, the reader and other readers and their cultural contexts, and so forth. Christians who read the Bible in this way can do so with their eyes wide open to all the influences that come into play as they hear its story. This doesn't mean that the Bible means whatever you or I say it does, only that reading the Bible is an encounter, an experience of the interplay of faith and reason, both of which are shaped by particular lenses through which one looks at the world.

Nor does it mean that what the Bible says didn't happen. To go back to our example, the fact that our knowledge of the debate over social security is filtered at several levels does not mean it did not actually happen. Here is where liberal interpreters of the Bible have a tendency to throw out the baby with the bathwater. To say that biblical writers wrote from a particular worldview or mind-set that shaped their writings is not the same thing as saying that they invented the events they were describing. An open-minded reading that rejects literalism doesn't force one to conclude that the Bible has no grounding in actual events in history or that because the gospels report Jesus' words through a lens, the writers made up the words.[7] Further, while all readings are subjective, some have the weight of consensus on their side more than others. John Cobb says, "The recognition that every theory is conditioned by the perspective of the thinker can be deeply internalized without the rejection of theological work or denial that some theories are better than others."[8]

Here is where the community of faith plays such an essential role. The church is the context for any reading of the Bible. Otherwise we read without the benefit of the insights and wisdom of other thinking both past and present. All interpreters need to hear how other people are understanding the stories that speak of God's judgment, love, and mercy as told in scripture. Open-minded

Christians don't need the church to tell them what they have to believe about the Bible, but they do need to listen to all voices within the church in order to experience the truth that "two are better than one" (Eccl. 4:9) when it comes to hearing and understanding the story of God that the Bible tells.

Authority is an inside job.

We have not yet provided a direct answer to the question of what an open-minded Christian can believe about biblical authority. Indeed, can the Bible have any real authority for us unless we believe that it was written by God? Is literalism, and its related doctrine, infallibility, necessary for one to believe that the Bible speaks with authority? These are important questions, and the answers given in the past have not been wholly satisfactory.

The more liberal reading of the Bible uses *descriptive* rather than *prescriptive* readings of scripture, making authority mostly a church matter about which interpreters need not be overly concerned. In essence, this perspective sets aside the issue of biblical authority in favor of boundless research into other matters. It has little concern for the relationship between the church and the Bible except as it existed in the first century.

A fundamentalist reading, on the other hand, sees no problem in *prescriptive* interpretations, defining the Bible as the word of God not subject to human qualification or alteration. This perspective puts one at the edge of the slippery slope that elevates a single point of view to being the only acceptable one. Perhaps worse, though, it literalizes metaphors and then turns them into doctrines that become tests of faith. This morning the sun came up, but, of course, it didn't. "The rising sun" is a metaphor that describes a reality but is not the reality itself. A fundamentalist view is that the sun's rising is reality.

Neither of these ways of viewing authority offers much help in understanding the role of the Bible today for those Christians who want to take it seriously but not literally. An alternative, however, can be forged between the appropriateness of an unrestricted search for truth (the former) and the conviction that the Bible speaks with authority (the latter). Here again Wright's work offers special insight. He likens biblical authority to a five-act Shakespearean play with most of the last act lost. Someone arbitrarily writing the fifth act is thought to be inappropriate because it would give Shakespeare responsiblity for work not his own. The solution is to give the roles in the play to highly trained actors well-versed in Shakespearean drama who would, in effect, immerse themselves in the language and culture of Shakespeare's day and then work out a fifth act for themselves. What would be the results? Says Wright:

> The first four acts, existing as they did, would be the undoubted "authority" for the task in hand. That is, anyone could properly object to the new improvisation on the grounds that some character was now behaving inconsistently, or that some sub-plot or theme, adumbrated earlier, had not reached its proper resolution. The "authority" of the first four acts would not consist —could not consist!—in an implicit command that the actions should repeat the earlier parts of the play over and over again. It would consist in the fact of an as yet unfinished drama, containing its own impetus and forward movement, which demanded to be concluded in an appropriate manner. It would require of the actors a free and responsible entering in to the story as it stood, in order first to understand how the threads could appropriately be drawn together and then to put that understanding into effect by speaking and acting with both innovation and consistency.[9]

Wright understands the biblical story in precisely this way: five acts, so to speak, consisting of (1) creation (2) the fall, (3) Israel, (4) Jesus, and (5) both the writing of the New Testament, including the gospels, and the church's "improvisational performance of the final act as it leads up to and anticipates the intended conclusion."[10] Herein lies the key to biblical authority. The New Testament is part of God's story begun at creation, sustained through the fall, continued in Israel, fulfilled in Jesus, and reaching all the way to Christians today who "love and serve the Lord" as a way of announcing the ultimate conclusion of what God has done. Biblical authority is in a sense the Bible's power to remind all Christians of the need, purpose, and effect of God's work in the world. For this reason Christians in every generation have been and are obliged to know the story scripture tells, and to know it well, to ensure that their proclamation of this story and the way they live it out in their time are consistent with the intent and content of the Bible. In short, the Bible is the overarching story within which the continuation of the story in our time is to be told. We are not free to tell the story as if nothing has been told before now. What we say requires a faithful continuation of the story that reaches back to the creation of the world.

In many respects this view of biblical authority reflects the very process by which the Bible as canon was developed. *Canon* means "standard." When the canon of sacred writings was established, the church was saying to itself and to the world, "These are the books that set the standard for all books that claim to tell the story of God's covenantal relationship with Israel and God's covenantal relationship with all people through Jesus Christ." All other books extant at the time had to "measure up" to the standard set by those in the Bible. In a sense, then, biblical authority is simply an acceptance of certain books as setting the measuring rod, or canon, by which the faithfulness of any witness to the continuing story of God's saving work is to be determined. The reason the books in the Bible emerged with this kind of authority was less the church council's choosing them and more their possessing the power to lead people to recognize their story as being bound up with God's story, and in that recognition to experience in one form or another "something like scales" falling from their eyes (Acts 9:18). Thus, the validity of the content of the story told by every generation is tested by its capacity to speak a word of life consistent with the word of life found in scripture.

Essentially, then, scriptural authority is all about obedience. The Latin root of the word *obedience* means "to listen to." The Bible's story confronts every generation with the question of whose voice to listen to amid the competing stories that seek to explain and/or offer life. In every generation people have listened to the biblical story, been changed by it, and then confirmed the authority of the Bible in the way they live their lives. At the same time, biblical authority functions this way only for those people willing to come to the Bible in faith. Faith and obedience are inextricably woven together. Faith opens one to experience the Bible's claim of authority on one's life. That experience serves to deepen one's faith. In this interface both the external (the Bible) and internal (choosing to become part of the story) dimensions of authority are at work.

An open-minded understanding of biblical authority, then, accepts the Bible as the standard by which appeals to any other kind of authority are to be measured, whether it be church tradition, reason, or personal experience, all of which have functioned as sources of authority within the church's life. What the church says and what an individual may understand or experience have significance only as they serve to complete the story told in the Bible, not to hold Christians captive to the past but to hold any single Christian perspective accountable to being consistent with the early church's witness. Otherwise, any generation of Christians can become a cut flower, without roots to sustain its growth to maturity. New insights into the story the Bible tells are always possible, and no one need fear what such insights might be or where they might lead. Indeed, the story continues for precisely this reason. But it is not just any story, or even our story. It is God's story we are to tell, and the Bible is the standard by which we can judge the faithfulness of our telling it in our own time and place.

Inspiration is the breath of God then and now.

Another question all of this raises has to do with the inspiration of scripture. In order to appreciate biblical inspiration we first need to be careful not to link it with literalism or infallibility, as is often the case. Rightly understood, the inspiration of scripture stands on its own quite apart from these two troublesome doctrines. It affirms both that the Holy Spirit was at work in the lives of the writers, leading them to tell the truth they knew in what God had done in Israel and in Jesus Christ, and that this same Spirit brings the truth of the Bible to life for people today as they read, study, and proclaim it. This means that inspiration is not only about something that once happened; it is about something that continues to happen. We don't have to believe it happened to someone else. We can experience it for ourselves.

In 2 Timothy 3:16–17 we read, "All scripture is inspired by God and is useful for teaching, for reproof, for correction, and for training in righteousness, so that everyone who belongs to God may be proficient, equipped for every good work." We can only assume that the word *scripture* in this text is a reference to the writings of the Old Testament, because the New Testament was a work in process at the time. But the point is, the inspiration of scripture is not an end in itself, but a means to an end. It serves the purpose of instruction and training in order to help Christians live and serve the Lord more effectively. It can do this because scripture is the very breath of God to the Christian. That's what inspiration means— that God breathed scripture. The same thing is said about the creation of human beings: "God formed man from the dust of the ground, and breathed into his nostrils the breath of life; and the man became a living being" (Gen. 2:7). It can be said of human beings that we are the inspiration of God. We make God known, even as we are fallible and imperfect, because God has breathed life into us.

To believe in the inspiration of scripture means, then, that God has breathed life into the words human beings wrote. They don't have to be perfect or infallible to make the word of God known, even as human beings do not have to be perfect in order to be vessels for making God known in the world. In the deepest sense the Bible is a living word. This is why it still exists. It hasn't lasted because someone said it was the word of God or declared it be infallible. It has lasted because of its power to breathe new life into people. If you have ever experienced reading a passage in the Bible and having the words you are reading suddenly take on life as you have never known them to have before, you have tasted of the inspiration of the scripture. The same thing can be said of hearing a sermon that lifts your spirit or stirs you into making an important decision. The Holy Spirit is at work in you through the proclamation of the biblical message.

Trusting the inspiration of scripture, then, is both possible and important, challenging any dismissal of it or efforts to add unnecessary doctrine to it. God breathed life into human beings, and God has breathed life into the words of human beings. Think of the Bible not so much as the inspired word *of* God, but an inspired word *from* God, a living word, to those who have faith in its truth and power.

2

What You Can Believe about Jesus

Jesus was a man.

Some people believe that the church has already spoken on the matter of who Jesus was in its creedal statements that have since become the bedrock for Christian belief.[1] At the same time the matter of what the ancient creeds mean continues to be a subject of much debate. Moreover, large numbers of Christians do not belong to creedal congregations and have little knowledge of them. To ask who Jesus was—and is—therefore, is to invite a discussion on an issue that goes to the heart of what it means to be Christian, but that is far from a settled matter.

It would seem that saying Jesus was a man would be something on which all Christians might agree, and on one level this is the case. But from the beginning it has been a point of controversy. Early in the life of the church some Christians adopted a corrupting influence on their understanding of Jesus called Docetism. These docetic Christians believed that God could not have contact with matter, and therefore, it was inconceivable that Jesus was the incarnation of God in human flesh. Instead, they said, he only appeared to be truly human, a heavenly being of sorts who took on

15

the appearance of being a man but who did not actually suffer and die as other Christians were claiming.

Docetism proved to be short-lived, but its passing by no means settled the matter of what Christians actually mean in saying that Jesus was a man. Indeed, there continues to be a tendency— consciously or unconsciously—to reject the full humanity of Jesus by placing exclusive emphasis on his divinity, something we will discuss later. For now we are concerned with the fact that such an emphasis creates the impression that Jesus did not live with the limitations that go with being human. If that were true, then the Docetists were correct: Jesus could not have been fully a man without living within the full range of possibilities and limitations that go with being human. The gospel of John provides an unequivocal affirmation of the humanity of Jesus when it declares, "And the Word became flesh and lived among us, and we have seen his glory, the glory as of a father's only son, full of grace and truth. (John testified to him and cried out, 'This was he of whom I said, "He who comes after me ranks ahead of me because he was before me."') From his fullness we have all received, grace upon grace" (1:14–16).

This statement is explicit in its insistence that Jesus was a man in the fullest sense of what that means. One marvelous benefit of this fact is that his humanity is the point of contact between our lives and his. The Jesus of stained-glass windows is too removed from the world we live in to have much meaning. The meaning of the Incarnation, that is, God's becoming flesh and dwelling among us, begins with Jesus' being fully human. In his humanity he was the completion of the salvation story that God began in Israel. Jesus was God's Word that became flesh. The key word is became. John does not say the Word came in the flesh. He says the Word became flesh. The focus is on the human form of God's story. The reality of human limitations did not prevent God from "speaking" the story of salvation for all humanity in the man Jesus.

In practical terms a profound meaning emerges from this reality. It is that Jesus knew who he was within the limits of being human. There is reason to assert that he was divine, as we shall see in a moment, but his own awareness of his divinity was within the boundaries of being human. In other words, Jesus and God did not sit down in heaven and discuss the plan of salvation and then Jesus came down to Earth to fulfill it, knowing every step of the way what was going to happen. If that were true, the Docetists had it right. Jesus would have been a divine actor who knew all along that he was in control of the events surrounding him. At any moment he could have changed what was happening. But that would make trusting the gospels harder because they would be witnessing to a charade of sorts in which God was playing a cosmic trick on the human race, a kind of "catch me if you can" game in which Jesus knew when he could be caught and when he could not be.

This is important because it serves neither the enrichment of personal faith nor the cause of Christ to attribute to the man Jesus knowledge about himself that renders his humanity void. The weaknesses of our humanity reveal the extent to which we fall short of being faithful followers of Jesus. The comfort we have in faith is not only trusting in God's forgiveness but also in believing that Jesus fully understands our struggles because he has, as we say, "been there, done that." The writer of Hebrews states it this way: "For we do not have a high priest who is unable to sympathize with our weaknesses, but we have one who in every respect has been tested as we are, yet without sin" (4:15).

Jesus has been there, and by that fact God has declared that it is okay that we are human beings. That is especially good news, because the alternatives are quite limited. It is not a bad thing to be human. We might even go so far as to say that being flesh and blood is actually a good thing, not because we are good, but because God came to us in the form we know very well, the human form. Believing that Jesus was a man goes to the heart of the good news he brought in his flesh and blood. His humanity is not incidental. It is essential, a statement that this God "in flesh" is one who walks and eats with the rest of humanity, who even washes the feet of others, and in doing so reveals "that it is all right to be human. That God knows we are human, and full of evil, and we are his people anyway, and the sheep of his pasture."[2]

Jesus was a man. This is where following him as Savior and Lord begins, because this is where it began with the first disciples. Everything else can follow from this very important affirmation.

Jesus is more than a man.

The verb in the subtitle above is in the present tense, whereas the statement about Jesus being a man is in the past tense. There is a reason for both. The humanity of Jesus has to do with who he *was* in flesh and blood. The divinity of Jesus, which is what saying he was more than a man refers to, has to do with who he *is*. The former is a statement of fact. The latter is a statement of faith. For Christians, of course, they carry equal weight and are not always clearly distinguishable. For the sake of clarity, the past and present tenses are being used to underscore the point that anything beyond saying Jesus was a man steps into the realm of faith statements. Thus, to say I believe that Jesus is more than a man actually says as much about me as it does about him, which is the way it is in matters of religious convictions.

There are Christians, of course, who are uncomfortable with distinctions between fact and faith, especially in regard to who Jesus was. For them the virgin birth stories found in the gospels of Matthew and Luke are proof positive that Jesus was the divine Son of God. By that they usually mean he was God. But believing that Jesus was more than a man is not the same thing as accepting the virgin birth stories. Let me explain.

The virgin birth narratives, as they are called, describe the way in which Jesus came into the world, whereas believing that Jesus is the incarnation of God speaks to the way in which he was and now is in the world. One can believe in the Incarnation whether one accepts or doesn't accept the virgin birth accounts. This is, in fact, what Christians have done from the very beginning of Christian history. Only two of the four gospels say anything about the virgin birth. Neither Mark nor John mentions it. In none of the gospels does Jesus himself say anything about it. There is no reference to it in the Acts of the Apostles or in any other book in the New Testament. Yet the belief that Jesus was more than a man, that he was the Son of God, the revelation of God, runs throughout the New Testament. We do not know if the story of Jesus' being born to a virgin was known to any of the other New Testament writers or was known but not considered important, but the absence of any reference to it at least suggests that their faith in him as the Son of God did not rest on believing in the virgin birth.

The reason is that Incarnation is the church's way of talking about the mystery of Jesus' identity. As the great theologian Karl Barth once said, in the person of Jesus, we encounter "the humanity of God."[3] Jesus as a man was also God in human form. To believe that is to accept mystery as part of the Christian gospel. We are not talking about Jesus' being a man who was used by God for a mighty purpose. We are not even talking about Jesus as the messiah of Israel, though as Christians we can believe he was, albeit not in the way first-century Judaism was expecting. We are instead daring to say that Jesus is God's Word made flesh. To see him through the eyes of faith means to believe that we are seeing what God is like, seeing clearly the will of God, the mind of God, the compassion of God, the love of God, in him.

The Jesus of John's gospel says this about himself:

> "Whoever has seen me has seen the Father. How can you say, 'Show us the Father'? Do you not believe that I am in the Father and the Father is in me? The words that I say to you I do not speak on my own; but the Father who dwells in me does his works. Believe me that I am in the Father and the Father is in me; but if you do not, then believe me because of the works themselves." (Jn. 14:9–11)

In his person and in the works he does, Jesus reveals God. This conviction led the ancient church to declare in its creedal formulations that Jesus was "fully human, fully divine."

Yet none of what we have said is an argument against believing that Jesus was born of a virgin, only that one can believe he is more than a man without it. To believe that he is more than a man means accepting Jesus as a revelation of what God has in store for the whole of humanity. Further, believing that he is more than a man is not a belief that Christians must explain fully for it to have validity. Rather, to speak of Jesus as being fully divine is to touch on the mystery of his nature, which the church has spent centuries trying to understand but has never been able to explain fully. Sometimes the more people try to explain mystery, the more they succeed in simply explaining it away. The nature of faith is to be willing to go beyond reason and logic, in a sense to be willing to walk off the end of the map into uncharted territory that can be known only by stepping into it.

The real task is to try to balance believing Jesus was a man and believing he is more than a man. Those who claim a "high christology," meaning they believe Jesus was divine, often make the mistake of defending this position by assigning Jesus special knowledge about himself that no human being could possess. This road leads to one of two alternatives: one either rejects Jesus' divineness or caves in to the doctrine of Docetism discussed earlier. But neither belief balances humanity and what I prefer to call Jesus' *otherness*. Such a balance can be achieved, however, by a single affirmation: *Jesus was more than he knew himself to be.*

There is no reason to assume that the *otherness* of Jesus required of him knowledge about himself he could not possess if he were fully human. There is every reason to believe he was more than he could have known about himself; in fact, to believe otherwise would destroy his humanity. This unawareness of his *otherness* can be seen in the temptation stories in all three synoptic gospels. Jesus goes into the desert after his baptism and is tempted to claim power and glory no human could possess. In Jesus' rejecting the lure of the tempter, the story is saying that he used what is available to all God's people in discerning the particular claim God has on them—prayer, fasting, scripture.

The way in which Wright explains this tension between Jesus' being both a man and more than a man is termed *vocation*. What Jesus knows about himself, his *otherness,* if you will, is vocational knowledge, which Wright describes as "risky" knowledge, not unlike knowing that one is loved.[4] He argues that Jesus believed he was called to fulfill the reign of God on earth, to be the embodiment of that calling, to be in fact a living symbol of it that challenged the cherished symbols of his day.[5] In short, he discerned his vocation. Had he known all along, even before his desert experience, who he was and what he was to do, the temptations would make no sense. As Wright puts it:

> "Awareness of vocation" is by no means the same thing as Jesus having the sort of "supernatural" awareness of himself, of Israel's god, and of the relation between the two of them…Jesus did not, in other words, "know that he was god" in the same way that one knows one is male or female, hungry or thirsty, or that one ate an orange an hour ago.

Further,

> As part of his human vocation, grasped in faith, sustained
> in prayer, tested in confrontation, agonized over in further
> prayer and doubt, and implemented in action, he believed
> he had to do and be, for Israel and the world, that which
> according to scripture only YHWH himself could do
> and be.[6]

This is a Jesus modern Christians not only can believe was
Savior but also can know as Lord. He was a man, but he is more
than a man. The son of Mary and the Son of God, limited as we are,
yet more than he knew himself to be. In the end, perhaps, this
reality is less explainable than it is proclaimable. Certainly the scales
of the New Testament witness are tipped in this direction. It would
seem that the church has not improved on this strategy.

Jesus was a teaching prophet, not a prophetic teacher.

The word *rabbi* means "master." In first-century Palestine it did
not refer to an official office but was a term of respect and deference
used for those Jews who were schooled in the law of Moses.
Although there is no evidence of his being trained in the law, Jesus
certainly engaged in teaching. The gospels present him as a teacher
of the masses. The Sermon on the Mount (Mt. 5—7) and the
Sermon on the Plain (Lk. 6:17–49) are but two examples of this
portrayal. Yet it is only in Mark and John that the term *rabbi* is
actually applied directly to Jesus (Mk. 9:5; 11:21; 14:45; Jn. 1:49;
3:2; 4:31; 6:25; 9:2; 11:8; 20:16), and even then in a limited
fashion.

This is curious because today Jesus is widely viewed primarily as
a teacher. This is true for Christians and non-Christians, no doubt
in part because it a role with which people today are familiar and
can easily understand. So even among Christians the primary
perception of Jesus is that he was a teacher of a new way of life. He
might have disturbed the status quo with some of the things he said,
but good teachers sometimes do that. Yet the designation *teacher*
cannot be limited to Jesus. John the Baptist was called "rabbi" by his
disciples (Jn. 3:26), and his teaching certainly stirred the water of
both first-century Judaism and Roman authority. But John's

followers did not become a lasting community as did the followers of Jesus, except that they might have become Jesus' disciples at John's death. The point, though, is that calling Jesus a teacher seems quite inadequate in capturing the way he was understood by those who knew him or by himself. Another perspective is needed. For help we once again turn to Wright.

He argues that a more encompassing view is that Jesus stood in the tradition of a prophet. In the Old Testament there are three words that describe one who is a prophet. The first two are usually translated "seer," the third *(nabi)* "prophet," meaning "one who is called to speak." The books of the prophets contain moving stories of these prophets' being called to speak on behalf of God to the people of Israel. Their primary theme was faithfulness to God over against the pagan gods around them. Prophets also spoke of a new day that would come, a time when God would restore the kingdom to Israel and reestablish the temple in Jerusalem as the dwelling place of the presence of the one true God. But this message was laced with words of judgment against the people of Israel for abandoning God and "whoring" after false gods to appease those who ruled over them. A biblical prophet, then, announced a new age dawning that would turn things upside down, that would require full obedience to the God of Israel and no other.

There is evidence that Jesus thought of himself in this way, but with an important twist. In Luke's gospel we read the following passage:

> When he came to Nazareth, where he had been brought up, he went to the synagogue on the sabbath day, as was his custom. He stood up to read, and the scroll of the prophet Isaiah was given to him. He unrolled the scroll and found the place where it was written:

> > *"The Spirit of the Lord is upon me,*
> > *because he has anointed me*
> > *to bring good news to the poor.*
> > *He has sent me to proclaim release to the captives*
> > *and recovery of sight to the blind,*
> > *to let the oppressed go free,*
> > *to proclaim the year of the Lord's favor."*

And he rolled up the scroll, gave it back to the attendant, and sat down. The eyes of all in the synagogue were fixed on him. Then he began to say to them, "Today this scripture has been fulfilled in your hearing." (Lk. 4:16–21)

In this text Jesus defines himself as one in whom Isaiah's words have come to completion. Thus, he was a prophet, *but no ordinary one,* rather, one who not only announced but embodied the actions of God for which Israel had long awaited. Wright notes that while other prophets announced the coming reign of God, Jesus enacted, symbolized, and personified that climactic event.[7]

> Forget the "titles" of Jesus…forget the pseudo-orthodox attempts to make Jesus of Nazareth the second person of the Trinity;…Focus, instead, on a young Jewish prophet telling a story about YHWH returning to Zion as judge and redeemer, and then embodying it by riding into the city in tears, symbolizing the Temple's destruction and celebrating the final exodus. I propose, as a matter of history, that Jesus of Nazareth was conscious of a vocation, given him by the one he knew as "father," to enact in himself what, in Israel's scriptures, God had promised to accomplish all by himself.[8]

Why is understanding Jesus as a prophet, but not just any prophet, important to an open-minded Christian? Two reasons. First, it is a reasonable way to hold in balance his humanity and divinity, of claiming that as a man he was more than he knew himself to be. Second, it points beyond his crucifixion to the necessity of the resurrection as the cornerstone for the church's life and witness. Jesus the man is the point of identity for people in general. Jesus the resurrected Lord is the point of identity for Christians in particular.

There is nothing original about sin.

For Christians the concept of salvation, to be discussed later, is an answer to the pervading human dilemma of sin. Saint Augustine, the Bishop of Hippo in Northern Africa (fourth century), is responsible for the concept of original sin. Augustine believed that sin came into the world through the first man and woman, Adam and Eve. The second creation story in Genesis 2:5—3:24 tells of their willful deviance of God's command not to eat of the fruit of the tree of the knowledge of good and evil. Woman, tempted by a serpent, eats the fruit, then persuades Man to do the same thing. Their willful defiance of God is what Augustine called the original sin, because its effects were like the ripples from a rock thrown in a pond. The seismic shift of the plates underneath the ocean that cause a tidal wave better fits the way Augustine interpreted this event. The entire human race was affected or infected, as the case may be, by the indiscretion of the first man and woman.[9]

Augustine interprets the apostle Paul's theological understanding of the creation story:

> Therefore, just as sin came into the world through one man, and death came through sin, and so death spread to all because all have sinned—sin was indeed in the world before the law, but sin is not reckoned when there is no law. Yet death exercised dominion from Adam to Moses, even over those whose sins were not like the transgression of Adam, who is a type of the one who was to come. But the free gift is not like the trespass. For if the many died through the one man's trespass, much more surely have the grace of God and the free gift in the grace of the one man, Jesus Christ, abounded for the many.

> And the free gift is not like the effect of the one man's sin. For the judgment following one trespass brought condemnation, but the free gift following many trespasses brings justification. If, because of the one man's trespass, death exercised dominion through that one, much more surely will those who receive the abundance of grace and the free gift of righteousness exercise dominion in life through the one man, Jesus Christ.

> Therefore just as one man's trespass led to condemnation for all, so one man's act of righteousness leads to justification and life for all. For just as by the one man's disobedience the many were made sinners, so by the one

man's obedience the many will be made righteous.
(Romans 5:12–19)

Jesus is the answer, says Paul, to the corruption and condemnation
of humankind that occurred in the first woman and man of
creation. It took that much for God to overcome the damning effect
of the fall.

It is an attempt to explain the inexplicable, this concept of
original sin. But in all candor it is not something Christians need to
believe per se. We can believe or not believe, and it won't matter one
whit in being Christian. Salvation in Jesus certainly doesn't depend
on it. The church existed for four centuries before Augustine's
brilliance and stature as a theologian and church leader won the day
on this issue.

Nor does taking the reality of sin seriously depend on believing
in original sin. What truly matters is that sin is real, and that it
corrupts human life. More importantly, it matters that sin requires
an antidote greater than "people trying to do better." Augustine was
on to something in recognizing the eternal significance of human
rebellion against God that the Genesis story describes. The real
world of daily living makes painfully clear the devastating effects of
human beings wanting to be God rather than believing in God.
Nuclear weapons poised to destroy the whole of human life,
terrorists piloting airplanes into buildings and killing thousands of
people, children bearing children, children killing children, adults
abusing children and each other, millions living in luxury while
even more millions live in abject poverty—the signs of sin are all
around. It's Sin with a capital *S*. The theological name is not original
sin. It is idolatry, of the kind we mentioned earlier in discussing
humanity's bearing the image of God. The writer of Genesis puts
the truth before us: Human beings are part of the creation, not the
Creator. We bear the image of God, and often try to be God, but
we are not God.

Not even Christians are exempt from this temptation, which is
why the apostle Paul speaks a truth anyone can understand when he
also writes to those Roman Christians,

> I do not understand my own actions. For I do not do what
> I want, but I do the very thing I hate. Now if I do what I

do not want, I agree that the law is good. But in fact it is no longer I that do it, but sin that dwells within me. For I know that nothing good dwells within me, that is, in my flesh. I can will what is right, but I cannot do it. For I do not do the good I want, but the evil I do not want is what I do. Now if I do what I do not want, it is no longer I that do it, but sin that dwells within me. (Rom. 7:15–20)

This is the human predicament, which is why Christians follow Jesus Christ. He is the assurance of forgiveness even as we confront being human. Call it original sin. Call it a flawed nature. Call it whatever we will, but scripture simply calls it sin. It is a reality.

Jesus' crucifixion was more than the death of a good man.

Traditional Christian theology says Jesus' death and resurrection offer a remedy to the problem of sin. That is, "in Christ God was reconciling the world to Himself" (2 Cor. 5:19). But why the cross? Why a death? How is it that his death was anything more than the death of a good man? In short, why did God do this? The church wrestled with these questions from the beginning, and by the fourth century four dominant views of "the doctrine of atonement," the name by which this struggle came to be known, had begun to emerge.[10] None of them is adequate in itself, and each overlaps with the others, but together they offer a broad outline of how Christians have generally interpreted the meaning of the death of Jesus. Therefore, it can be helpful to summarize each of the perspectives.

The first is the Latin view, which says that in dying on the cross, Jesus earned sufficient merit to appease the anger of God toward a sinful humanity. Such merit could be earned only by one who was without sin. Thus, God sent Jesus for this purpose. He came to die for an undeserving humanity hopelessly lost without God's justice being satisfied.

The second doctrine of atonement is the sacrificial view. It declares that God required a sacrifice in the tradition of the sin offering practiced in Israel to absolve humanity of its guilt. Again, because of humanity's corruption God sent Jesus to be this sacrificial offering. He was "the blood of the Lamb," as termed in traditional hymns, that appeased the anger of God and made forgiveness possible.

A third view is the "moral example" interpretation of Jesus' death. Jesus is understood as being the embodiment of divine love that revealed the extent to which God was willing to go to reclaim humanity. So compelling was this demonstration of divine love that men and women are drawn to it and inspired to live at a higher moral level themselves.

The fourth view is the classical perspective. Jesus' death is seen as the final and victorious act of God to defeat the power of evil in the world. Jesus' coming to earth was God's invasion into Satan's realm to defeat him and set humanity free from the bondage of evil and its accompanying hopelessness that seemed unconquerable. This defeat foreshadowed the final triumph of righteousness and justice soon to come and the joining together once again of God and the whole of creation.

What all these various views have in common is the belief that Jesus' death was a decisive event in God's saving work on behalf of all humanity. The dominant view in the church has been the sacrificial interpretation. Jesus died on behalf of a sinful humanity in order for God to forgive us. His death was a reconciling moment between God and humankind, made possible by Jesus' being the unblemished sin offering: "in Christ God was reconciling the world to himself, not counting their trespasses against them…For our sake he made him to be sin who knew no sin, so that in him we might become the righteousness of God" (2 Cor. 5:19, 21).

Yet to many open-minded Christians this way of understanding the death of Jesus raises many questions. Why would God need the death of Jesus to forgive when throughout the Old Testament there are references to God's being a forgiving God? "When deeds of iniquity overwhelm us, you forgive our transgressions" (Ps. 65:3). It is precisely this kind of troubling issue that gave rise to other views of atonement in the first place. But in their own ways, each has led to a view of Jesus that has either made him even more removed from human experience (the classical view) or nothing more than a good example to follow (the moral example view).

I want to suggest another way. Since in the end all the doctrines of atonement we have mentioned point to a common theme—that sin is a serious problem in the divine/human relationship—the way for open-minded Christians to move beyond the limits that the theme suggests is to focus on what the Bible says is the ultimate source of all sin—idolatry. This is the sin of sins, which is why the first of the Ten Commandments says, "I am the LORD your God, who brought you out of the land of Egypt, out of the house of slavery; you shall have no other gods before me" (Ex. 20:2–3). It is why Jesus told his disciples to seek the reign of God first in their lives, after which all other things would have their place (Mt. 6:33). Thus, it is reasonable to believe that Jesus died for precisely this reason. Human beings are given to idolatry. He came as one who embodied a new reality, and in him God was doing a new thing for Israel and all humanity (Isa. 42:9); the promise to Abraham (Gen. 12:3) that through his seed Israel would become a blessing to the nations was now being fulfilled. But the people would not listen. The blindness of Jewish leaders and the power of Rome combined to exact Jesus' death. From this perspective the cross is a symbol of humanity's self-condemnation. God did not send Jesus to die. God sent Jesus to be "the bread of life" (Jn. 6:35). But the circumstances of first-century Palestine were such that the Jewish leaders in Jesus' day failed to recognize that through him God was making a new visitation (Lk. 19:44).

But what makes it possible for us to speak of forgiveness—and this is the crucial point—is the resurrection. It is the reason there are Christians at all, something we will examine in detail in a moment. Doctrines of atonement discuss the crucifixion as if it could have meaning in and of itself. As we shall see, this is not the case at all. It is the hope that the resurrection of Jesus represents that makes his death more than a tragedy. Indeed, it is because of the resurrection that open-minded Christians can understand the death of Jesus as a redemptive act. Without the resurrection, the crucifixion of Jesus would have been lost to history. Because of it, his cross stands as a poignant symbol of the cost of sin.

For open-minded Christians, then, when the question is asked, Did Jesus know he was going to die? the answer must be no if saying yes means he possessed knowledge that made him something more or less than human. But the answer can be yes if it means he knew he was going to die based on his discernment of the circumstances in Jerusalem at the time and his understanding of the consequences to which those circumstances could lead.

Idolatry. This was the sin with which Israel always had to contend. It continues to be for all humanity. Willful and persistent sin was and is the ultimate rejection of God's sovereignty. In Jesus' death, the death of one flawlessly faithful to God, God for that moment turned away from Israel and humanity. Further, because humanity is an extension of God as Creator, Jesus' death was in reality God turning away from God's self, a kind of self-rejection reflected in the anguish Jesus expressed when he cried out, "My God, my God, why have you forsaken me?" (Mt. 27:46; Mk. 15:34).

This is the cry of God suffering on behalf of a people God had graciously invited into covenant. The crucifixion of Jesus was the ultimate death penalty for Israel and all humanity brought about by human folly. The mystery of it is that it is a judgment God chose to take on God's self in the person of Jesus. It was the flood story all over again, only this time God kept the promise not to destroy the whole of humanity. Instead, God gave up a Son who "humbled himself and became obedient to the point of death—even death on a cross" (Phil. 2:8). The crucifixion was the inevitable consequence of sin, divine judgment, and condemnation that pierced God's heart. It is the fulfillment of the truth that "the wages of sin is death" (Rom. 6:23).

The resurrection is more than an empty tomb.

Jesus' death was real, and it was devastating to his disciples. Their grief had to be profound. That is the way it is when someone we believe in dies. To this day I feel the pain of the day President Kennedy was assassinated. So, too, with the deaths of his brother Robert and Martin Luther King, Jr. These were men I believed in, believed were making the world a better place for all people. But evil killed them, and for me it seemed that hatred had won the day. Jesus' disciples had to feel that way when he died. His death confirmed the power of Rome over their lives, a cruel and gruesome reminder of who really held power.

In his autobiography, Nelson Mandela tells the story of his fight for freedom for all South Africans, black and white alike.[11] The book humanizes the struggle, especially the devastating impact his sentence to life in prison had on him, his wife, his children, his friends, and the African National Congress, of which he was the primary leader. Because we know the fight for freedom was finally won, and South Africa stands today as a model of a democratic state genuinely committed to justice for all, we can overlook the pain and agony Mandela's imprisonment for twenty-seven years created not only for him and his family but for his followers.

This is a crucial dimension of the death of Jesus. The power of the resurrection begins in the recognition of the trauma his death caused for those who had been following him. They huddled in grief and agony in what has come to be called the upper room, wondering what to do next. Part of the reason they met after his death must have been to console one another. Part of the credibility of the resurrection of Jesus lies in the fact that it was these same grief-stricken people who shortly thereafter began to speak openly and boldly about it.

> The cross and the resurrection…are clearly central to virtually all known forms of Christianity. But the rise of that early Christian understanding is only comprehensible on the basis that certain things continued to be known, as history, about the one who (among so many others) was crucified outside Jerusalem and who (unlike any others before or since—a fact of some significance) was declared by his followers to be alive shortly afterwards. The resurrection vindicates *what Jesus was already believed to be;* it cannot be the sole cause of that belief which sprang up around it.[12]

The second thing to say about the resurrection is that it is the core belief of Christianity.

> The confession of Jesus as resurrected, as living with God's own life, and as ruling as Lord of the church and the world is what distinguishes the Christian view of Jesus from every other view. For everyone else, Jesus is another dead man; for Christians, he is the Living One. This confession is implicit in the very existence of the church gathered in Jesus' name, in its celebration of the Lord's Supper, in its healing in the name of Jesus, in its struggle against evil for the little ones with whom Jesus identifies himself.[13]

Without Jesus' resurrection, then, there would be no church, Jesus would in all likelihood be forgotten, and world history would be a different story altogether. The resurrection is not simply an important thing to believe in. As a Christian it is *the first thing* to believe in. Recently, a new Christian told me that he didn't really care that much about life after death and that he had a lot of questions about the resurrection of Jesus. My response was that he needed to realize that his struggle was focused around the very thing without which he would not even have had the chance to become a Christian. The heart and soul of Christianity is that Jesus was raised from the dead. It was recognized as such from the very beginning:

> Now if Christ is proclaimed as raised from the dead, how can some of you say there is no resurrection of the dead? If there is no resurrection of the dead, then Christ has not been raised; and if Christ has not been raised, then our proclamation has been in vain and your faith has been in vain. We are even found to be misrepresenting God, because we testified of God that he raised Christ—whom he did not raise if it is true that the dead are not raised. For if the dead are not raised, then Christ has not been raised. If Christ has not been raised, your faith is futile and you are still in your sins. Then those also who have died in Christ have perished. If for this life only we have hoped in Christ, we are of all people most to be pitied. But in fact Christ has been raised from the dead, the first fruits of those who have died. (1 Cor. 15:12–20)

The reason the resurrection is the cornerstone of Christianity is that it is the sign of divine forgiveness and the victory God has won over evil. As the crucifixion was an act of human folly, the resurrection was God's forgiveness for that act. It was the final statement of divine love that declared death would not separate humankind from God, because God forgave sin. "The wages of sin," Paul says, "is death, but the free gift of God is eternal life in Christ Jesus our Lord" (Rom. 6:23). This is the choice of God, to forgive humanity's idolatrous and disastrous ways. Paul says it clearly and best when he writes:

What then are we to say about these things? If God is for us, who is against us? He who did not withhold his own Son, but gave him up for all of us, will he not with him also give us everything else? Who will bring any charge against God's elect? It is God who justifies. Who is to condemn? It is Christ Jesus, who died, yes, who was raised, who is at the right hand of God, who indeed intercedes for us. Who will separate us from the love of Christ? Will hardship, or distress, or persecution, or famine, or nakedness, or peril, or sword?

No, in all these things we are more than conquerors through him who loved us. For I am convinced that neither death, nor life, nor angels, nor rulers, nor things present, nor things to come, nor powers, nor height, nor depth, nor anything else in all creation, will be able to separate us from the love of God in Christ Jesus our Lord. (Rom. 8:31–35, 37–39)

The resurrection is also more than having faith.

All the above points to the validity of believing in the resurrection of Jesus. But it doesn't answer all the questions. What was the nature of it? What kind of body did he have? Even with faith in the resurrection these are issues not to be ignored, primarily because there are sensible answers to them. The church need not fear being queried about these matters. Besides, asking questions may not be a sign of a lack of faith. It may arise from a desire to find some solid ground on which to stand when quizzed by others.

At the same time, open-minded Christians will want to proceed with caution in confronting such questions. We must avoid the temptation to make claims about the resurrection that easily break down when challenged. One example is declaring that Jesus was raised because the tomb was empty and that no one has ever found his body. This is what in logic is called a *non sequitur*. It is "a statement that does not follow logically from what preceded it." It is true enough from all the accounts we have that the tomb of Jesus was empty three days after his crucifixion. But that doesn't necessarily mean that he was raised from the dead. The gospel of Matthew tells us that some Jewish leaders went to Pilate, the Roman governor, and told him of their concern that Jesus' followers would steal his body and then claim he had been raised. Pilate agreed to let them place guards at the tomb to prevent this from happening (27:62–66). One scholar even claims that one of the men crucified with Jesus was a doctor who helped Jesus and himself survive by placing some healing medicine on their wounds; later, Jesus escaped to Syria and lived to an old age.[14] As far-fetched as this may seem, it illustrates how far people will go to show that an empty tomb is not reason enough to believe Jesus was raised.

The fact is that the gospel accounts tell much more about what happened. They report an empty tomb but also describe some of Jesus' disciples meeting him face-to-face. Women meet him outside the tomb. Two walk with him on the road to Emmaus. He appears to them in the upper room, the second time inviting Thomas the doubter to put his finger in his wounds. He meets them on the seashore and eats breakfast with them. He meets Saul of Tarsus on the road to Damascus, and Paul later tells us that Jesus appeared to more than five hundred followers. This is more than a story about an empty tomb. It is the life-changing experience of Jesus' first-century followers. When they began to tell others about what happened to them, the church was the result. People responded with faith and experienced their lives also being changed.

This is the heart of believing in the resurrection. Jesus is alive. As one testimony states it:

> "Christ is alive," I said to myself. "Alive!" and then I paused: "Alive!" and then I paused again: "Alive!" Can that really be true? Living as really as I myself am? I got up and walked about repeating, "Christ is living! Christ is living!" At first it seemed strange and hardly true, but at last it came upon me as a burst of sudden glory; "Yes, Christ is alive." It was a new discovery.[15]

These words are the witness of a famous British minister, who goes on to say, "I thought that all along I had believed it; but not until that moment did I feel sure about it. I then said, 'My people shall know it. I shall preach it again and again until they believe it as I do now.'"[16]

Jesus is alive. *He* was raised from the dead. Not his ideas. Not his dream of a new Israel. Not the concept of God's unconditional love that he showed in his actions. Jesus was raised to new life. This is unambiguously the story of the New Testament. Later generations have believed or not believed it, but that the man Jesus known by his disciples in the flesh was raised from the dead is without question the witness of the New Testament. An open-minded Christian can trust that the weight of logic is on the side of belief. It is less than convincing to think that Jesus' followers put their lives on the line for something they knew to be untrue. It would not matter much if they believed that his ideas and teachings were sufficiently compelling to warrant being written down and taught to a new generation. This preposterous story was simply an unnecessary complication for the first Christians. Nothing in their Jewish heritage would have led them to make such a claim. The only logical reason for it was that they met the living Jesus. They saw him, talked to him, ate with him, and in the end understood that their mission was to tell others the good news that death was not the last word. Life was. Obviously his body was different in a mystical way from his body before the crucifixion. He appeared and disappeared. But the gospels are quite clear in saying that Jesus appeared in a bodily form his disciples knew to be his. This is the reason they preached that he was the Messiah, the Christ for whom the Jews had been waiting. Their faith in Christ was born out of their experience with the bodily resurrected Jesus whom they had followed.

Salvation is a gift of God.

Salvation is the church's term for the effect of the crucifixion and resurrection of Jesus. But what we have said up to this point may have raised questions about what it actually means to speak of salvation in Jesus Christ. Have we blurred the distinction between the categories of *saved* and *lost,* or do these terms have any real meaning any longer? For some Christians the distinction is unequivocal. Believe in Jesus and you are saved. Don't believe and you are lost. Being saved means going to heaven. Being lost means going to hell.

It would be easy to reject this approach to salvation as too simplistic, if not self-righteous. Further, it would seem that Jesus himself rejected it, as his parable of the Pharisee and the tax collector suggests:

"Two men went up to the temple to pray, one a Pharisee and the other a tax collector. The Pharisee, standing by himself, was praying thus, 'God, I thank you that I am not like other people: thieves, rogues, adulterers, or even like this tax collector. I fast twice a week; I give a tenth of all my income.' But the tax collector, standing far off, would not even look up to heaven, but was beating his breast and saying, 'God, be merciful to me, a sinner!' I tell you, this man went down to his home justified rather than the other; for all who exalt themselves will be humbled, but all who humble themselves will be exalted." (Lk. 18:10–14)

This story is obviously a warning about the temptation of self-righteousness, but it also implies that certainty about who is in and who is outside the mercy of God is specious. Jesus makes a similar point when he warns:

"You have heard that it was said, 'You shall love your neighbor and hate your enemy.' But I say to you, Love your enemies and pray for those who persecute you, so that you may be children of your Father in heaven; for he makes his sun rise on the evil and on the good, and sends rain on the righteous and on the unrighteous." (Mt. 5:43–45)

Yet it can also be said that rejecting outright the notion of people being "saved" and "lost" fails to address the question of divine judgment. It rightly highlights the grace of God, but neglects the need for divine justice. The interpretation of the crucifixion and resurrection discussed earlier seems to me to strike a balance between mercy and justice, judgment and forgiveness. It takes evil seriously, but trusts in the ultimate triumph of good. But does it offer salvation to all regardless of what they believe? The answer is no, because that is not the issue it addresses. Rather, crucifixion as judgment and resurrection as forgiveness focus on the need to resist the temptation of making salvation dependent on human response. Simply stated, while believing that salvation is the gift of God in and through Jesus is basic to Christian faith, Christians have tended to take the next step and make God's salvation dependent on faith in that belief. It is not surprising that in the process we have limited the benefit of God's salvation to those who believe in it. Human response to God matters, but God's salvation has happened in Jesus whether it is accepted or not. Acceptance means one can celebrate it. Acceptance is not what makes it possible.

We shall discuss the implications of this statement in the chapter on what open-minded Christians can believe about other religions. For the moment the point is that salvation is truly the gift of God. It does not depend on one's believing in it for it to be true, because it is something that occurred before we were born. As the apostle Paul states, "But God proves his love for us in that while we still were sinners Christ died for us" (Rom. 5:8). Open-minded faith is careful not to confuse the action of the gift-giver with the reaction of the recipient. Rejecting a gift does not change what the gift-giver has done. It does diminish the effect the gift has in one's life, but it does not alter the fact that the giving of the gift does not depend on merit or contrition.

But some may object that this turns God's demand for justice into mush or that it makes obedience unnecessary. As to the first charge, Paul must have also heard it. He responds in this way:

> What then are we to say? Is there injustice on God's part? By no means! For he says to Moses, "I will have mercy on whom I have mercy, and I will have compassion on whom I have compassion." So it depends not on human will or exertion, but on God who shows mercy. (Rom. 9:14–16)

Paul wanted the Christians in Rome to understand that salvation was solely an act of God, independent of human response. Human response would always be inadequate to gain salvation; it literally took an act of God for salvation to become possible.

Judgment is better than we think.

Because of the resurrection, and only because of it, God's judgment is better than what the church has generally said about it. This does not mean that divine judgment is to be taken lightly, only that there is much confusion about it, in large part because of the fact that the church has used it as a way to maintain power. To dispense or withhold forgiveness has been one of the church's major weapons in its arsenal of authority. To understand why judgment is better than you might think, we need to look afresh at what scripture says about it.

The New Testament speaks of the judgment of God in the context of what is called *eschatology*, or those things that have to do with "end times." It is generally assumed that this is a reference to the end of the world, but Wright and others argue that the first Christians were more likely to have associated "end times" with the restoration of Israel, seen in the question the disciples ask the resurrected Jesus, "Lord, is this the time when you will restore the kingdom to Israel?" (Acts 1:6). This would most certainly fit both the Old Testament concept of God's coming judgment and the expectations of first-century Judaism. But in all instances the point of divine judgment is to save, not to condemn, to generate new devotion to God, not to cut down. This is the key element of the judgment of God we must understand. Its purpose is to save, to redeem, to transform, to bring about changes that produce faithfulness and life.

There are, of course, consequences to our actions from which neither God nor anyone else can exempt us. The apostle Paul describes it as reaping what we sow, harvesting what we plant (Gal. 6:7). Unfortunately, others may also suffer from our mistakes and foolishness, from our sin. It is judgment in the Old Testament tradition, what can be called *existential judgment*. But even then the redemptive dimension can be present. When bad things happen, people have the opportunity to make a new start, to be rehabilitated. That some do not has more to do with their choices than with the absence of a redemptive moment.

But eschatological judgment is another matter. It has to do with consequences God has already redeemed in the crucifixion and resurrection of Jesus. That is what we call divine grace. From a Christian perspective eschatological judgment involves humankind's not receiving what we deserve, not experiencing final condemnation even though that would be justice. End-time judgment is good news judgment, because God has already declared us forgiven in the person of Jesus. Does this mean you can go out and do whatever you want to? Of course not.

What then are we to say? Should we continue in sin in order that grace may abound? By no means! How can we who died to sin go on living in it? Do you not know that all of us who have been baptized into Christ Jesus were baptized into his death? Therefore we have been buried with him by baptism into death, so that, just as Christ was raised from the dead by the glory of the Father, so we too might walk in newness of life. (Rom. 6:1–4)

No one who has experienced the grace of God in Jesus Christ will want to abuse that gift. Such a desire is a sign that a true encounter with Jesus has not occurred. Judgment is better than we think precisely because it gives us the desire to be different.

Forgiveness is at the same time awful and wonderful.

Believing that divine judgment is better than we might think is no reason to think that forgiveness is handed out like candy to children. Forgiveness is an awful thing to go through. It begins when we face up to the need for it, which means being painfully honest about an attitude or action that has injured someone else or perhaps even our relationship to God. We have become adept at wearing masks and hiding the truth about ourselves not only from others but also from ourselves. Forgiveness cannot be experienced until the mask is stripped away and we see the truth we have gone to great lengths to avoid. This is why forgiveness cannot be coerced. Receiving it depends on being open to it, which in turn allows us to experience the power of it.

It is not unlike having a debt forgiven or wiped out. Years ago a generous man loaned me money to pay off a school debt; then he unexpectedly forgave it. It was a humbling and at the same time wonderful experience. My step was definitely a little higher when I walked out of his office that day. I did nothing to receive this act of generosity. It was solely his decision. Had I turned the gesture down, I would have missed experiencing the power of what he did. My acceptance did not make his gift possible, but it made my life different. Simply stated, forgiveness is both an awful and wonderful experience. What is more, it is something we can experience over and over again, and the freshness of the taste is never lost. We are tempted to think it will be, but Jesus assures us that it will be fresh even after receiving it seventy-seven times (Mt. 18:22).

Heaven and hell are more than places to go.

To grasp the biblical meanings of "heaven" and "hell," we need first to remember a point already made—metaphors lose their power and relevance when they are literalized. When the Bible speaks of heaven and hell as "places" to go, it is consciously using metaphorical imagery to express realms of existence not intended to be understood as actual places in spatial terms. When the writer of Revelation described heaven as a place with pearly gates, streets of gold, and mansions in the sky, he hardly intended those to whom it was written to think of the dwelling place of God in such materialistic terms. Equally the case, when he wrote about the lake of fire into which those who reject the Lamb will be cast, he didn't intend his readers to think of a lake burning as if oil had been spread across it. The dwelling place of God is, he says, with people (Rev. 21:3), which should not be surprising, because the climactic moment in history is one that takes place on earth (vv.1–2).

A deeper and more helpful way to understand the biblical metaphors of heaven and hell is to understand the former as *living in* the presence of God, the latter as *living outside* that presence. To be in the presence of God is to be "in heaven." Heaven is "the dwelling place" of God. If, then, God is never in one place but is everywhere at once—what theologians call omnipresent—then heaven is not a place, but the presence of God.[17] To go to heaven would, therefore, more accurately mean to be in God's presence. This is eternal life. In contrast, hell is the absence of divine presence. Moreover, it is being conscious of that absence. It is, as one parable describes it, being tormented by the awareness that one is looking over a great chasm but cannot pass from one side to the other (Lk. 16:19–31).

Living in the presence of God is a fundamental promise in scripture. To Moses, who is commissioned to go back to Egypt, God promises, "I will be with you" (Ex. 3:12). To the people ready to enter the promised land, Moses speaks these words, "It is the LORD who goes before you. He will be with you; he will not fail you or forsake you. Do not fear or be dismayed" (Deut. 31:8). To Joshua after Moses' death, God promises, "As I was with Moses, so I will be with you; I will not fail you or forsake you" (Josh. 1:5). This is the most basic promise God made to the people. At the same time, the loss of God's presence is the most dreaded of punishments. Again, Moses warns the people, "For the Amalekites and the Canaanites will confront you there, and you shall fall by the sword; because you have turned back from following the LORD, the LORD will not be with you" (Num. 14:43). As a contrite King David begs, "Do not cast me away from your presence, and do not take your holy spirit from me" (Ps. 51:11).

The presence of God, what Judaism called the Shekinah, was Israel's protection and comfort. God's Shekinah meant that God cared for them, that they were loved, forgiven, and safe. In short, it was heaven, not a place to go to, but a state of existence in which to dwell. So the tent of the Presence came to symbolize this reality; later it was the Jerusalem temple, and still later the person of Jesus Christ. He was the presence of God in the flesh. Salvation in him is the full expression of this gift of divine presence, because his death and resurrection expunge the notion that God's presence is conditional or limited by time and space. It is eternal, everlasting, unending, because God is everlasting to everlasting. Moreover, through Jesus this gift is extended to all peoples.

This is salvation, a state of being, a way of living. To think in terms of place is a human effort to describe the indescribable, to express in words limited by time and space what is eternal. Ascribe to it all the metaphorical beauty you can imagine. It is worthy of such praise. But remember that all words are limited metaphors of that which no words can fully capture, for that of which we speak is the very presence of the Holy One, Creator of heaven and earth and all that dwells therein.

If this is what heaven is, living in the presence of God, then what we have said about hell must also be taken seriously. It is separation from God, living with a mind and heart alienated from God. This kind of living is not something God intends or imposes. It is in the fullest sense self-imposed, a result of exercising one's right to choose to reject God. In order for heaven to be real, hell must also be real. Believe in both of them. The former is a gift of God; the latter is the consequence of rejecting that gift. Each in its own way affirms the sovereignty of God and the reality of the consequences of human choice.

Miracles are a sign of God's future in the present.

The gospels tell us that Jesus performed many miracles. The blind are made to see; the lame are made to walk; the sick are made well; even the dead are raised. They also tell us that he did such things as walking on water and turning water into wine at a wedding feast. How trustworthy are these stories? Are such miracles to be believed as actually having happened? It will help in finding an answer to this question to look at what the Bible means by the word *miracle*.

There are two Hebrew words for miracle used in the Old Testament. One is *oth*, which is usually translated "sign"; the other is *mopheth*, which is translated "wonder." These are synonyms and often occur together in the same text, such as in Exodus 7:3 where God tells Moses, who cannot speak well, that he will send his brother Aaron with him to speak for God and tell Pharaoh, "I will multiply my signs and wonders in the land of Egypt," in order to convince the Egyptian ruler to let the people of Israel go. There are many other passages in which "signs" and "wonders" occur in the same text (Deut. 4:34; 6:22; 7:19; 13:1; 26:8; 28:46; 34:11; Neh. 9:10; Ps. 105:27; Isa. 8:18; Jer. 32:20; Dan. 6:27). As used in these passages, a sign is something that points to God, whereas a wonder is special evidence of God's power. A wonder can serve as a sign that may point to a future event that God will do. At the same time, wonders were not always signs of God's power. Israel is explicitly warned about false prophets claiming to perform divine wonders:

> If prophets or those who divine by dreams appear among you and promise you omens [signs] or portents [wonders], and the omens or the portents declared by them take place, and they say, "Let us follow other gods" (whom you have not known) "and let us serve them," you must not heed the words of those prophets or those who divine by dreams; for the LORD your God is testing you, to know whether you indeed love the LORD your God with all your heart and soul. (Deut. 13:1–3)

A similar use of the two words is found in the New Testament, with sign *(semeion)* understood as a miracle that is taken as evidence of divine authority. This is the case in the gospel of John, which is sometimes called the "sign gospel." John portrays Jesus as performing seven miracles that point to his being God's Word in the flesh and worthy of their belief in him. The gospel reflects the fact that the early Christians did not view the universe from the perspective of the natural and supernatural, as is the case today. In their world no such distinction existed. Miracles did not evoke a need for explaining how the supernatural could controvert established natural law. The tension between the two simply did not exist. In the gospels, Pharisees come to Jesus requesting he provide a sign that he is from God: "Then some of the scribes and Pharisees said to him, 'Teacher, we wish to see a sign from you'" (Mt. 12:38; see also 16:1). His disciples make a similar request (Mt. 24:3). Signs and wonders producing awe and belief were common expectations.

Things changed, of course, as we began to learn more about the world we inhabit. Responding to this changing perspective, theologians began to posit various views to explain miracles. Some said that humans did not possess sufficient knowledge to understand that miracles did not contradict natural law but were part of the created order, and that this reality would someday show itself to be the case. Others argued that there was a closed natural order, but that God sometimes intervened in what humans labeled the miraculous. The pure naturalist worldview rejects any suggestion that divine intervention is real. Miracles are simply and solely that which lies in the eye of the beholder.

What can we believe about any of this? One thing is that none of this matters in terms of believing that Jesus was the Son of God. Miracles fall into the same category as the virgin birth. One's faith is not at stake one way or the other. Christians have stood on both sides of the debate over miracles. That being said, believing in them is more than superstition. C. S. Lewis, for example, accepted the reality of miracles. He was convinced that they were part of God's created order and were not interventions at all. The problem was the limited, finite mind of human beings that could not comprehend the supernatural coexisting with the natural order. He saw miracles as portals to God's order and God's future. They were the unfolding of the future in the present.[18] The word that describes this approach to miracles is *proleptic.*It means to taste the future in the present. It may help you to think of miracles in this way. They are a taste of God's future in the here and now. They reveal something in part that will become fully known at a later time. In this sense the resurrection of Jesus was proleptic, a breaking in of the natural order to point to that which God intends for the whole of humanity. Miracles, then, can be seen as signs of hope rather than tests of faith. One can be a believer and not believe in miracles, but to believe in them is to claim in the present a moment whose fullness is yet to come.

Communion is not just a supper.

It is because of the resurrection, and only this, that the church gathers around the communion table. In this act the church witnesses to a faith that in one respect believes in the resurrection and in another has that trust vindicated by the mystical experience of the presence of the raised Jesus in the gathering. In the deepest sense communion is the moment when faith and action come together to confirm each other. Coming to the table expecting to meet Jesus makes it possible for that to happen. It may not happen every time, because we are not always ready to experience him. But it can happen, even every time. This is what Paul is saying in his description of Jesus' instructions about this special meal:

> For I received from the Lord what I also handed on to you, that the Lord Jesus on the night when he was betrayed took a loaf of bread, and when he had given thanks, he broke it and said, "This is my body that is for you. Do this in remembrance of me." In the same way he took the cup also, after supper, saying, "This cup is the new covenant in my blood. Do this, as often as you drink it, in remembrance of me." For as often as you eat this bread and drink the cup, you proclaim the Lord's death until he comes. (1 Cor. 11:23–26)

The word *remembrance* in both Hebrew and Greek means to recall an event in such a way as to become a participant in it.[19] He is inviting his followers to experience afresh sitting at the table with him. Paul tells the Corinthian Christians that this is what Jesus said about communion after Paul sternly rebukes them for becoming so filled with wine they could not experience the presence of Jesus in the act of breaking bread as the church (11:20–22).

The church has maintained the practice precisely because of Jesus' words. We may not always sense the presence of Jesus, but we can believe that he is present, and in believing we wait for him to make himself known to us: "When he was at the table with them, he took bread, blessed and broke it, and gave it to them. Then their eyes were opened, and they recognized him" (Lk. 24:30–31).

Helping the poor is more than lending a helping hand.

The Lord's supper is not the only way you can test out the resurrection for yourself. Jesus promised that he would meet his followers in the poor:

> "Then the righteous will answer him, 'Lord, when was it that we saw you hungry and gave you food, or thirsty and gave you something to drink? And when was it that we saw you a stranger and welcomed you, or naked and gave you clothing? And when was it that we saw you sick or in prison and visited you?' And the king will answer them, 'Truly I tell you, just as you did it to one of the least of these who are members of my family, you did it to me.'" (Mt. 25:37–40)

Jean Vanier is the founder of L'Arche ("the Ark"), a community for the severely mentally and physically disabled. It started in 1964 when he invited two young men, Raphael and Felipe, whom he had met through a priest friend, to leave the institution in which they were being housed and come live with him. Today there are 117 such communities around the world, places where the most vulnerable and rejected in society are loved and valued. Vanier describes them as teachers of the powerful and the strong about the ways of the heart. The seeds of L'Arche were planted when this great man, according to his own testimony, "left the [British] Navy in 1950 to follow Jesus."[20] He found him when he met Felipe and Raphael.

The presence of the raised Jesus can be experienced in many ways today, and each one confirms the truth of this fundamental Christian claim. According to Jesus' own words he will always be found among the poor, the weak, and the vulnerable. This is not only something we can believe. It is something about which we need never have a doubt.

— 3 —

What You Can Believe about God

God really is.

Everything we have said thus far rests on one very large presupposition—that God actually exists. Some people, of course, reject the existence of God. It is a choice they make, because faith and doubt are always choices. But is there any logical basis for choosing faith? Can faith and reason be partners in affirming the existence of God?

The place to begin is to realize how utterly profound believing in God is. It means first of all that one is a theist. This is a person who not only believes in the physical universe that can be observed and the life we as humans experience but also asserts that there is One who gives meaning and purpose to both the universe and human life. This means believing there is order to life, not chance, but design. As such, belief in God means affirming that intelligence rather than chance gave birth to the creation.

It is also reasonable to believe that any consciousness of what is right and wrong comes from God. In his World War II BBC radio talks to a beleaguered nation, C. S. Lewis sought to make a case that human nature, which he described as the awareness of a standard of right and wrong behavior to which all people appeal in one form or another, is in and of itself evidence of the existence of God. Different civilizations have not had different moralities, he said, but "only had *slightly* different moralities."[1]

> Think of a country where people were admired for running away in battle, or where a man felt proud for double-crossing all the people who had been kindest to him. You might as well try to imagine a country where two and two made five. Men have differed as regards what people you ought to be unselfish to—whether your own family, or your own countrymen, or every one. But they have always agreed that you oughtn't to put yourself first. Selfishness has never been admired. Men have differed as to whether you should have one wife or four. But they have always agreed that you mustn't simply have any woman you liked.[2]

In this same essay Lewis goes on to assert that the person who declares that she does not believe in any "real Right and Wrong" always goes back on it a moment later. She may break her promise to you, but if you break yours to her she will protest. He further asserts that not only is the awareness of a standard of right and wrong behavior universal but so is the breaking of it. These two concepts give human beings more than instinct or laws of nature by which to live. Instinct and laws of nature, he said (as previously noted), tell you what an object will do. Moral law, the law of human nature, on the other hand, tells you what people ought to do and not do. His conclusion is that the reality of moral law points to a reality beyond anything human beings have created. For Lewis, this reality was God.

The alternative to faith in God is to believe that God does not exist, that the universe and life arose by accident, and that any order to either is mechanical and without purpose or design. This essentially makes life one big crapshoot, so to speak, in which anything is possible and nothing is certain, where no standard of right and wrong can be appealed to except on an individual basis, which another can reject. In short, it declares that life is ruled by chaos and tempered only by the forces of raw nature and the survival of the fittest.

That is not the Christian view of life for one simple reason. A Christian makes the profound claim that God truly exists. That claim changes the way one looks at everything else.

God really is personal.

As we have said, it makes a significant difference whether or not a person believes in God. But what matters even more is the kind of God one believes in. One of my teachers used to say that it is easy enough for men and women to believe in God as long as they do not much care what kind of God. There is statistical evidence to support his assertion. Consider the following. In 1997, 95 percent of the American people said they believed in God. But when asked if they believed in a God who was an all-powerful, all-knowing, perfect Creator of the universe who rules the world today, that figure dropped to 68 percent. Of that number, 11 percent said the God they believe in represents a state of higher consciousness; 7 percent said God is the total realization of personal human potential; and 15 percent said God is no longer involved in their lives.[3]

These figures are significant, especially when they indicate that even though 95 percent of the population claims to believe in God, close examination reveals that only about 35 percent believe in the various images of God found in scripture. The God of the Bible is all-powerful and all-knowing, the perfect Creator of the universe who rules the world. But this God is much more than that. The God the biblical writers believed in was personal. This is the witness of both the Old and New Testaments. They speak of God in terms of One who can be known, loved, prayed to, and called on. Further, flowing naturally from such a belief is trusting that God knows you, knows your name, knows your life. As Jesus states, "And even the hairs of your head are all counted" (Mt. 10:30). Not to believe this is to place limits on your faith that cause you to miss the heart of believing in a personal God. If God can be known, then God can know your name.

The Sunday after a family of five started attending our church, my wife, Joy, happened to be in the hallway as they entered. Remembering the name of the four-year-old from the previous week, she said, "Good morning, Kayla," to which Kayla immediately responded, "You remembered my name! You remembered my name."

Knowing someone's name is an important dimension in all relationships. Relationships can never be personal until names are known. To believe in a God who is personal is to believe in a God who knows our names, who knows us. Such a God is clearly superior to one that is less than this. The reason is simple to see. Since we understand and know what it means to be human, and live by the conviction that human beings are the highest form of life on earth, to believe in a nonpersonal God, a "force" if you will, means believing in a God who is *less* than what humankind is. It makes more sense to believe that the Creator is at least equal to the creation, and in fact is much more. The biblical witness is to a God who created people for covenantal relationship with God's self. One is free to reject this concept of God, but the alternative is either to believe in a lesser God or not to believe at all.

But the primary reason Christians believe in a personal God is Jesus Christ. He was the incarnation of this personal God. He was—and now is—God with us, God pitching a tent among us (Jn. 1:14). One reason to believe God chose to act in this way is the fact that we can understand and relate to that which is human. As flawed and imperfect as we are, we can communicate with one another. It makes good sense, then, that God would communicate with us in this way, in a manner that would convey best the nature of God and God's will for us. This is the kind of God we can not only speak about but speak to, not only know about but know. Believing in a personal God is not without its problems, but to believe in a nonpersonal God has so many more, not the least of which is having to explain how human beings who are personal originated from that which is not. While the whole earth may declare the glory of God, it seems shortsighted to suppose that this is all we can say about God when what stands at the center of the creation is the most personal of all things—human beings. The appropriate desire to have done with masculine images of God that promote male hegemony or exclude women altogether does not warrant rejecting the personal God to whom scripture openly witnesses.

By definition Christians are those who believe that Jesus revealed the truth of God. That truth is that God is personal. "Of course, God is more than we are, but [God] must be at least *as much as* we are. The alternative to He or Thou is It."[4] Does this mean that

God is "a" person? The answer is obviously no. But leave out the article and the sentence conveys a bigger picture of God. God is Person. That is what personal means. Some theologians have resisted the step from saying God is personal to God is Person, but as one person says, this is like "a smile without a face."[5] The verb without the noun is meaningless. God is personal because God is Person, the Source and Creator of all persons.

God is not gender-neutral.

Some Christians believe that language about God used in the church is male-dominant, which excludes women. They advocate using gender-neutral names such as Parent or God rather than the pronoun *he* or the noun *Father*. Others think this is nothing more than the influence of feminist theology powered by the pressure of political correctness. I suggest that the answer is neither, but not because they are wrong. Quite the opposite. Both contain a measure of truth. It is true, for example, that the church's language about God is clearly male-dominant. The real problem, though, is not language for God, but rather the fact that male-gender language in general is used when more inclusive language would do just as well. *Humankind* would do quite well for *man* or *mankind*. *She* is just as useful as *he*. There are also occasions in which feminine images of God, such as *Mother*, would expand a congregation's perspectives on God. In short, the gospel would be better served if church leaders were more careful with language.

At the same time, gender-neutral terms, while politically correct in academic and judicatory circles, are theologically wrong because they undermine the personal nature of God, which we have pointed out as one of the basic claims of scripture. To refer to God as "the divine parent" is not only linguistically offensive, it challenges the personal dimension of the God/human relationship. To insist that a child refer to her mother as "parent" would change the nature of that relationship. That is the problem with gender-neutral language for God. It does precisely what the language itself intends. It creates the image of God as neutral, thus depersonalizing the human relationship with God. In this regard gender-neutral language is anything but.

Because God is personal, language for God should be personal. This is certainly what Jesus intended when he told the disciples to pray to God saying, "Our Father." The same could be said about using the noun *Mother* for God or *Father-Mother God*. A position between the two extremes would be one that argues that when it comes to God the challengers to male-gender language must be careful not to throw the proverbial baby out with the bathwater. Gender-neutrality is an absurdity when it comes to God. God is both male and female, not neither. Without concern for balance the push for inclusive language can be justly characterized as an effort to promote a feminist agenda, and the resistance to it as an insensitive traditionalism that wants its way no matter what. Neither does much to strengthen faith or present the gospel in a winsome way. God is Father. God is Mother. God is God. Thanks be to God![6]

God is "here" and "there."

Once open-minded Christians affirm that God is personal, the next step is to believe God is both immanent (here) and transcendent (there). The name given to this affirmation is *panentheism,* in contrast to *pantheism,* which claims that God is immanent only. In other words, God fills all of creation but is not distinct from it. Panentheism balances immanence and transcendence. God is expressed in creation but has identity apart from it. This belief allows for God's involvement in human history. In other words, it has room for the supernatural. If God exists, then God who created the natural world cannot be limited by it except as God chooses to be. Only if we determine that God cannot intrude on the natural order can we eliminate the possibility of miracle. But to say this means the creature can define the limits of the Creator. To claim faith and yet believe that God is nothing more than creation, or is limited by the natural order, is self-contradictory. There is a basic reason why, which is our next topic.

God is free to do whatever God chooses to do.

What this means is that God alone is sovereign. For centuries the Rock of Gibraltar off the southern coast of Spain has served as a symbol of what is certain and reliable. Open-minded Christians can believe this about the sovereignty of God without fear of giving up belief in human freedom. The sovereignty of God is something about which there is no equivocation in the Bible. God alone is sovereign. There is no equal to God. The God of Abraham and Sarah, Moses and David, Jesus and the first Christians, is sovereign. There is no other. The foundation of faith is that God is sovereign, the cornerstone, in fact, if not a veritable boulder.

The reason this is so important is because it means that God is free to do whatever God chooses to do. Jesus makes this abundantly clear in the parable of the workers in the vineyard (Mt. 20:1–15). Some workers labored all day, others half a day, still others only an hour, but they were all paid the same. Those who worked all day protested. The owner responded, "Friend, I am doing you no wrong; did you not agree with me for the usual daily wage? Take what belongs to you and go; I choose to give to this last the same as I give to you. Am I not allowed to do what I choose with what belongs to me? Or are you envious because I am generous?" (vv. 13–15).

Jesus said the parable was about the kingdom of God. As such it is about a sovereign God free to do what God chooses to do. Sovereignty means being free to make decisions as one chooses. Divine decisions reflect the divine will, which we can try to understand but must always accept. If God chooses to be equally gracious to all, that is God's choice. Any belief that limits God's freedom reveals a desire to make God into who one wants God to be. But it is God's nature to surprise us. The prophet Jeremiah declares that the Babylonians will be the instrument of God to destroy an unfaithful nation (22:20–22), but almost within the same breath speaks of a new covenant God will make with Israel that will never be broken (31:31–34). Priests throw a woman caught in adultery at Jesus' feet and with self-assuredness tell him what God expects them to do with her. But Jesus asks them to proceed only if there is one among them who is without sin (Jn. 8:7). That is the way of God—doing the unpredictable and unexpected because that is the way of One who alone is sovereign.

If there is anything we can say about God being consistent, it is that God chooses to act with compassion and forgiveness in precisely those ways and circumstances that are unpredictable. The prophet Isaiah understood this about God when he wrote, "For my thoughts are not your thoughts, nor are your ways my ways, says the LORD" (55:8). An earlier prophet, Samuel, even offered a reason why: "For the LORD does not see as mortals see; they look on the outward appearance, but the LORD looks on the heart" (1 Sam. 16:7).

According to scripture, however, there is one thing open-minded Christians can trust without fear—that God always errs on the side of love. Nothing in the Bible even hints that it is God's desire to punish or condemn humanity. Just the opposite. God has no desire to condemn the world, John's gospel declares, but God loves the world so much that salvation comes as a gift through the most unexpected way—a child named Jesus born to a young peasant woman (3:16–17). God is free to act in this way because God alone is sovereign. Not only is this something open-minded Christians can believe about God. There is no other "something" about God that is more important.

God is not a soft touch.

None of what we have said should lead to the conclusion that God is soft and expects nothing from us. That would be to confuse love for permissiveness. God always has and always will expect obedience from people. Moreover, there are consequences to disobedience (see the earlier discussion on judgment). It's called divine justice.

Obedience, if we remember, means "to listen." That is the essence of God's expectations of us. God expects us to listen, to pay attention, and for good reason. God is wiser than we are. Life has design. The universe has purpose. Loving God is our way of listening. This is what Jesus means when he answers the question, "Which commandment in the law is the greatest?" by saying, "'You shall love the Lord your God with all your heart, and with all your soul, and with all your mind.' This is the greatest and first commandment" (Mt. 22:36–38). He also adds that obedience includes not only loving God but also loving others: "And a second is like it: 'You shall love your neighbor as yourself.' On these two commandments hang all the law and the prophets" (39–40). Love is the content of obedience.

So is truth. In 1 Peter 1:22–23 we read, "Now that you have purified your souls by your obedience to the truth so that you have genuine mutual love, love one another deeply from the heart. You have been born anew, not of perishable but of imperishable seed, through the living and enduring word of God." Truth and love are two sides of the same coin. Listening to truth produces love. Following the way of love reflects the best truth we know. In an age when winning is more important than truth, whether in court or in a political campaign, open-minded Christians can be a witness to another way by believing in and devoting themselves to truth and love.

4

What You Can Believe about the Holy Spirit

The Holy Spirit is a lot more than a holy ghost.

It is unfortunate that the original King James Version of the Bible translated "Holy Spirit" as "Holy Ghost." Consciously or unconsciously, that is how many people of past generations came to think about it—a ghost in the sense of a being beyond the realm of human reality not to be taken all that seriously. This image was intensified by the general perception that the most visible expressions of the Holy Spirit were people writhing on the floor or speaking in a strange language no one understood, creating the suspicion that what passed for the Holy Spirit was nothing more than emotionalism without adequate restraints. What also added to skepticism about claims for the reality of the Holy Spirit were tensions and schisms within congregations over such matters as "praying in the Spirit" and "faith healing services" that grew up around what was labeled "the charismatic movement" in the 1970s and 1980s. In the end, though, the controversy and skepticism served to strengthen the rationalism that has come to dominate mainline Christianity since the eighteenth-century Enlightenment.

Yet studies suggest that people want something more than a rational faith. During this "charismatic" period of the last twenty to thirty years, during which mainline churches have experienced significant numerical decline, Pentecostal churches have been growing. Even when we factor in that this development has more than one cause, the conclusion one cannot escape is that people are looking for faith communities that can help them discover something more or deeper than a faith limited by scientific rationalism. This growth seems to be saying that people believe in the mystical dimension of faith and want help tapping into it. But what can we say about the Holy Spirit that speaks to this need without discounting rational faith altogether?

The first question to answer is, who is the Holy Spirit? Here scripture is quite clear. The Holy Spirit is God. In Genesis 1:1–2, for example, we read, "In the beginning when God created the heavens and the earth, the earth was a formless void and darkness covered the face of the deep, while a wind from God swept over the face of the waters." The word for "wind" is *ruach,* which is the same word used for "Spirit." So the text is saying that the Spirit of God moved over the face of the waters.

In Numbers 11:16–17 we read that God responded to Moses' plea for help in leading a disgruntled people with these words:

> So the LORD said to Moses, "Gather for me seventy of the elders of Israel, whom you know to be the elders of the people and officers over them; bring them to the tent of meeting, and have them take their place there with you. I will come down and talk with you there; and I will take some of the spirit that is on you and put it on them; and they shall bear the burden of the people along with you so that you will not bear it all by yourself."

Again, the word used here is *ruach.* When Zechariah was called to prophesy to the people of Israel, he was told he would do this ministry "not by might, nor by power, but by my spirit, says the LORD of hosts" (Zech. 4:6). Same word—*ruach.* The Holy Spirit is God. The work of the Holy Spirit is the work of God.

But the Spirit is also Jesus, because the Father and the Son are one.

"I have made your name known to those whom you gave me from the world. They were yours, and you gave them to me, and they have kept your word. Now they know that everything you have given me is from you; for the words that you gave to me I have given to them, and they have received them and know in truth that I came from you; and they have believed that you sent me. I am asking on their behalf; I am not asking on behalf of the world, but on behalf of those whom you gave me, because they are yours. All mine are yours, and yours are mine; and I have been glorified in them. And now I am no longer in the world, but they are in the world, and I am coming to you. Holy Father, protect them in your name that you have given me, so that they may be one, as we are one." (Jn. 17:6–11)

The Holy Spirit is God. The Holy Spirit is Jesus. It is the mystery the doctrine of the Trinity seeks to express, yet cannot explain. It is to put into words what scripture seeks only to name as reality without explanation. The Spirit underscores the mystical dimension to Christian faith.

But we can go further. The Bible also speaks of the work of the Holy Spirit. The Genesis text above, for example, declares that the Holy Spirit creates life. Jesus says the Spirit also creates new life. He calls it being "born again":

"Very truly, I tell you, no one can enter the kingdom of God without being born of water and Spirit. What is born of the flesh is flesh, and what is born of the Spirit is spirit. Do not be astonished that I said to you, 'You must be born from above.' The wind blows where it chooses, and you hear the sound of it, but you do not know where it comes from or where it goes. So it is with everyone who is born of the Spirit." (Jn. 3:5–8)

The Holy Spirit is a creating force for life. It is the "breath" of God in human beings and in the whole of creation.

The Holy Spirit also protects us. Matthew's gospel says that when Jesus was baptized, the Holy Spirit immediately led him into the wilderness where he was tempted by the evil one (4:1). This is the writer's way of saying that Jesus did not go into temptation alone. The Spirit was there to protect him, a promise we Christians can claim for ourselves as well. But what might this actually mean? One thing it might mean is that it can protect us from becoming a partner to the evil we may be seeking to overcome. Nelson Mandela tells about one of the commanding officers of Robben Island Prison, a Colonel Piet Badenhorst, who was especially harsh on him and his fellow prisoners. Mercifully, commanding officers came and went on Robben Island, and this was the case with Badenhorst. A few days before Badenhorst was transferred, Mandela was called to the main office where in front of Badenhorst he was quizzed by the commissioner of prisons about any complaints he or the other prisoners had. Not intimidated, Mandela went through an entire list of complaints and demands. When he finished, Badenhorst looked directly at him, told him he was leaving the island, and added, "I just want to wish your people good luck." Mandela was dumbfounded by what he said, and later wrote of the incident:

> I thought about this moment for a long time afterward. Badenhorst had perhaps been the most callous and barbaric commanding officer we had had on Robben Island. But that day in the office, he revealed that there was another side to his nature, a side that had been obscured but still existed. It was a useful reminder that all men, even the most seemingly cold-blooded, have a core of decency, and that if their heart is touched, they are capable of changing.[1]

These words are from a man who had twenty-seven prime years of his life unjustly taken from him. His experience as a Christian man serves as a reminder to all of us that the Holy Spirit will protect us in the worst times of our lives from the evil one who would have us to become the very thing we are fighting to overcome.

A third thing scripture says the Holy Spirit does is to serve as our tutor. In John's gospel Jesus says that the way the Spirit performs this function is by helping us to remember what he said: "I have said these things to you while I am still with you. But the Advocate, the Holy Spirit, whom the Father will send in my name, will teach you everything, and remind you of all that I have said to you"

(Jn. 14:25–26). The Holy Spirit stirs our memories so that in crucial times in our lives we remember something Jesus said or did that helps us to continue living as one who belongs to him. Perhaps this is also one of the ways the Spirit protects us. In a moment when we are being tempted to strike back, to become like our enemies, the Spirit stirs in us a memory of Jesus saying to love our enemies (Mt. 5:43–44) or to treat others the way we want them to treat us (Mt. 7:12). We can trust that each time we remember something Jesus said or did that helps us remain faithful to him, we are experiencing the work of the Holy Spirit.

A fourth thing scripture says is that the Holy Spirit confirms the gift of divine blessing. For example, in the passage previously cited (Num. 11:16–17), God responds to Moses' plea for help by conferring the blessing of leadership on the elders of Israel.

When King David commits adultery with Bathsheba and then has her husband Uriah, a trusted warrior for the king, put on the front lines, where he is killed in battle, the psalm of repentance traditionally attributed to him finds him pleading to God, "Do not cast me away from your presence, and do not take your holy spirit from me" (Ps. 51:11).

These passages speak of the blessing of the Holy Spirit being necessary for one to be able to lead the people of God. The absence of the Spirit or the losing of it both symbolize the absence of divine blessing.

Scripture also refers to the Holy Spirit as the source of power and strength to do all things, *including the forgiving of sin*. We are told that at the baptism of Jesus the heavens opened, and the Holy Spirit came upon him as if descending like a dove (Mk. 1:10). This same Spirit then led Jesus into the wilderness and strengthened him to resist the temptations to be disobedient to God (Mk. 1:12–13). At Pentecost this Holy Spirit came upon the disciples, enabling them to speak in their native languages and later to speak boldly about Jesus' being raised from the dead (Acts 2:1–15). After the resurrection the bestowing of the Holy Spirit on the disciples gave them the power to forgive sin: "When he had said this, he breathed on them and said to them, 'Receive the Holy Spirit. If you forgive the sins of any, they are forgiven them; if you retain the sins of any, they are retained'" (Jn. 20:22). We are not the source of the forgiveness. We are the announcers of it. We are the ones Jesus says can declare it to those who need to know this good news. By the power of his Spirit we can be faithful in this vocation.

Yet another way scripture says the Holy Spirit works is to enable believers to testify to Jesus as Savior and Lord under duress and even persecution.

> "As for yourselves, beware; for they will hand you over to councils; and you will be beaten in synagogues; and you will stand before governors and kings because of me, as a testimony to them. And the good news must first be proclaimed to all nations. When they bring you to trial and hand you over, do not worry beforehand about what you are to say; but say whatever is given you at that time, for it is not you who speak, but the Holy Spirit." (Mk. 13:9–11)

Not only this, but Paul says that even the power to profess Jesus as Lord comes from the Holy Spirit and that such a profession is a sign of the presence of the Holy Spirit: "Therefore I want you to understand that no one speaking by the Spirit of God ever says 'Let Jesus be cursed!' and no one can say 'Jesus is Lord' except by the Holy Spirit" (1 Cor. 12:3).

The Holy Spirit is also the source of the spiritual gifts Christians manifest in serving and witnessing to Jesus: "Now there are varieties of gifts, but the same Spirit; and there are varieties of services, but the same Lord; and there are varieties of activities, but it is the same God who activates all of them in everyone. To each is given the manifestation of the Spirit for the common good" (1 Cor. 12:4–7). These are the specific ways Christians make Jesus known. Spiritual gifts are many and varied, but they all share one purpose, which is to build up the church.

Finally, the Holy Spirit is referred to as one who produces fruits that witness to the presence of Jesus in the lives of Christians: "The fruit of the Spirit is love, joy, peace, patience, kindness, generosity, faithfulness, gentleness, and self-control. There is no law against such things" (Gal. 5:22–23). While Galatians seems not to be concerned with the order of these fruits of the Spirit, Paul identifies love as the essential and quintessential fruit when he writes, "And now faith, hope, and love abide, these three; and the greatest of these is love. Pursue love and strive for the spiritual gifts" (1 Cor. 13:13—14:1). Love is the fruit of the Spirit that confirms we are in the presence of a spiritual gift being exercised to build up the church.

In all these ways scripture assures us that the Holy Spirit is one who blesses our lives and empowers us to do what we could not otherwise do. Rather than a "ghost," the Bible speaks of the Holy Spirit as a real and tangible expression of God's presence and power in our midst.

Essentially, then, the Spirit is God in the world, but it also witnesses to Jesus as God in the world. At the same time, Jesus' life witnessed to the work of the Spirit. That is why the church speaks of God in three persons—Father, Son, and Holy Spirit. God is known in three ways. Each witnesses to the other.

The Holy Spirit makes baptism something more than getting wet.

All forms of baptism involve water: sprinkling, pouring, immersing. The latter involves the person's being placed fully under water and then raised up, symbolic of dying to the old and rising to new life. But much more is going on than getting wet. In the case of Jesus, baptism was the moment when the Holy Spirit was conferred on him. John the Baptist told the people listening to him that while he baptized with water, the One coming after him would baptize with the Holy Spirit and with fire (Mt. 3:11). Just before the baptism with the Holy Spirit happened at Pentecost, Jesus appeared to the disciples and assured them this promise would be fulfilled (Acts 1:4–5). Thus, scripture describes the conferring of the Holy Spirit as a baptism of a special kind. It was a baptism of power, as we have discussed, one that did not necessarily coincide with water baptism. The people of Samaria, for example, believed Philip's message about Jesus and were baptized with water, receiving the power of the Holy Spirit after some time had lapsed:

> Now when the apostles at Jerusalem heard that Samaria had accepted the word of God, they sent Peter and John to them. The two went down and prayed for them that they might receive the Holy Spirit (for as yet the Spirit had not

come upon any of them; they had only been baptized in the name of the Lord Jesus). Then Peter and John laid their hands on them, and they received the Holy Spirit. (Acts 8:14–17)

This was the crucial baptism. There are some Christians who seem to think that water baptism is the essential experience and even that a particular form (immersion) is necessary for salvation. Yet it is the baptism of the Holy Spirit that scripture suggests is the one without which water baptism means very little:

> While Apollos was in Corinth, Paul passed through the interior regions and came to Ephesus, where he found some disciples. He said to them, "Did you receive the Holy Spirit when you became believers?" They replied, "No, we have not even heard that there is a Holy Spirit." Then he said, "Into what then were you baptized?" They answered, "Into John's baptism." Paul said, "John baptized with the baptism of repentance, telling the people to believe in the one who was to come after him, that is, in Jesus." On hearing this, they were baptized in the name of the Lord Jesus. When Paul had laid his hands on them, the Holy Spirit came upon them, and they spoke in tongues and prophesied— altogether there were about twelve of them. (Acts 19:1–7)

This is not to say that water baptism is unimportant. Symbols are important in a faith community, especially one that points to conversion. Our point is simply that in the New Testament, Christian baptism involves much more than water. Baptism is being filled with the power of the presence of God in Jesus that makes effective witnessing possible. This is something especially important to believe about baptism.

The Holy Spirit's presence or power plays no favorites.

Jesus refused to allow boundaries and barriers erected by people to separate themselves from one another to rule his life. The first realization the early Christians came to was that neither did the Holy Spirit.

While Peter was still speaking, the Holy Spirit fell upon all who heard the word. The circumcised believers who had come with Peter were astounded that the gift of the Holy Spirit had been poured out even on the Gentiles, for they heard them speaking in tongues and extolling God. Then Peter said, "Can anyone withhold the water for baptizing these people who have received the Holy Spirit just as we have?" So he ordered them to be baptized in the name of Jesus Christ. Then they invited him to stay for several days. (Acts 10:44–48)

Gentiles were brought into the Christian community immediately, not by the disciples, but by the Holy Spirit. The disciples were, in fact, amazed by what the Spirit had done. Even after following Jesus for three years, their faith was still in a box. They were prepared to continue living by boundaries of the mind that maintained those external boundaries that segregated people by religion or race or color or nationality or gender. The church continues to struggle with the Holy Spirit's work in this regard. Because of the boundless nature of the community of Jesus the Spirit falls on people others do not think it should fall on.

This means that the Holy Spirit not only has no favorite people, but has no favorite gift to bestow. Early on some Corinthian Christians got the silly notion that speaking in tongues was the only genuine gift of the Spirit. The belief was an effort to mask sinful pride and arrogance. But Paul was an effective voice against such thinking, and the church today is the better for it.

The reason the Holy Spirit crosses temporal boundaries is the desire for unity among Christians, something for which Jesus himself prayed.

"And now I am no longer in the world, but they are in the world, and I am coming to you. Holy Father, protect them in your name that you have given me, so that they may be one, as we are one." (Jn. 17:11)

Unity in the community of Jesus. This is what the Holy Spirit is constantly seeking to bring about. It goes beyond modern ecumenism, which is the most visible effort today in bridging barriers that separate Christians. Unity stands over against any and all controversy that embitters Christians against one another and sends them into separate corners. The unity of the Trinity is symbolic of that which is intended for the community of Jesus called the church. We can be sure, therefore, that the Holy Spirit continues to nudge us toward visible manifestation of that reality so that the church might know the power that being one with Jesus and one another makes possible (Mt. 12:25).

We get the Holy Spirit's power the old-fashioned way.

There is a remarkable story in Acts about a man named Simon of Samaria who was a magician and then became a Christian in response to the preaching of Philip the evangelist. Curiously, the Holy Spirit had not yet come upon these new converts. When Peter and John came from Jerusalem to see the fruits of Philip's missionary work, they laid hands on them, and they were filled with the power of the Holy Spirit. Apparently Simon was not present at the time but was so impressed by the Spirit's power in these people (we are not told how it was manifested) that he offered money to the apostles to have it for himself. Peter sternly rebuked him for his gesture. This is how the text describes it:

> Now when the apostles at Jerusalem heard that Samaria had accepted the word of God, they sent Peter and John to them. The two went down and prayed for them that they might receive the Holy Spirit (for as yet the Spirit had not come upon any of them; they had only been baptized in the name of the Lord Jesus). Then Peter and John laid their hands on them, and they received the Holy Spirit. Now when Simon saw that the Spirit was given through the laying on of the apostles' hands, he offered them money, saying, "Give me also this power so that anyone on whom I lay my hands may receive the Holy Spirit." But Peter said to him, "May your silver perish with you, because you thought you could obtain God's gift with money! You have no part or share in this, for your heart is not right before God. Repent therefore of this wickedness of yours, and pray to the Lord that, if possible, the intent of your heart

may be forgiven you. For I see that you are in the gall of bitterness and the chains of wickedness." Simon answered, "Pray for me to the Lord, that nothing of what you have said may happen to me." (Acts 8:14–24)

Peter's rebuke seems a bit harsh. Nothing in the story suggests that Simon's conversion was not genuine. Further, his effort to "buy" the Spirit's power only confirms his need for spiritual growth and, thus, his true need for the Spirit's power working in his life.

Herein is the lesson we can take from this story. We know that the power of the Holy Spirit cannot be bought, but the deeper truth is that the power of the Spirit cannot be had without a cost. That cost is attentiveness to it. Essentially, the Spirit's power works by invitation. It falls on anyone who truly wants it. We can even say that it is never absent, but it is sometimes, even many times, underused. Jesus tells us to ask for what we need, and it will be given to us (Mt. 7:7–8). He doesn't say it might be granted or sometimes will be. He says it *will* be granted, going further and saying that it would be unthinkable for God not to respond to our needs:

> "Is there anyone among you who, if your child asks for bread, will give a stone? Or if the child asks for a fish, will give a snake? If you then, who are evil, know how to give good gifts to your children, how much more will your Father in heaven give good things to those who ask him!" (Mt. 7:9–11)

This is not a passage about getting what we desire for ourselves. Jesus made it clear to the mother of James and John that making inappropriate requests would be dealt with by God (Mt. 20:20–23). It is about the power available to Christians that often goes unused. The work of ministry is not powered by us, but by the Holy Spirit. But the Spirit does not force itself on us. It comes by invitation.

What we are talking about is the place that prayer should play in our lives. It is the way we position ourselves to receive the Holy Spirit on a daily basis. Or to change the image, it is the way we allow the Holy Spirit to be released from within to do what only the Spirit can do. Whatever the image, the thing to remember is that the Holy Spirit has power to help us live and move and have our very being as disciples of Jesus, but it is a power we claim, not one that intrudes without invitation. It works this way because of free will. God has chosen to give humankind freedom of choice. The Holy Spirit works within this reality. But we are assured that the power of the Spirit is ours for the asking.

5

What You Can Believe about Moral Questions

This may be a bit tongue in cheek, but it makes a serious point:

Even in theory, the notion that reasonable people can differ is a bit lame. On matters you're confident you're right about, it is surely bewildering how others can differ. The temptation is to assume they must be stupid or dishonest, and that is often true. But often it is patently not true. So you wonder; I am not gifted with superhuman vision. Why don't all reasonably intelligent and honest people see things the way I do?

They could of course be blinded by prejudice or predisposition. I think this is often the case, especially about politics. Intelligence and honesty are sometimes no match for comfortable habits of thought...It's possible, I charitably suppose, for even fair-minded people not to realize how wrong they are.

The distressing corollary of this generous thought is that I might be one of these misguided people. I don't think so— but then I wouldn't, would I?

In ordinary times, even the professional opinionizer learns to live with the mystery of how other people can be so wrong. But when so many others, some whose honesty you respect...seem in all sincerity to believe the unbelievable, that induces epistemological vertigo.[1]

Nothing among Christians is more common than "epistemological vertigo," a spinning of the head due to intellectual bewilderment, only we hardly ever realize that is what we are experiencing. We usually think it is frustration (and perhaps fatigue as well) caused by people who refuse to see how wrong they are about something or other. Being absolutely sure of our point of view, it strikes us as totally enigmatic that others could think whatever it is they are thinking or believe whatever it is they believe. Thus, epistemological vertigo.

This chapter may make this problem worse for you, though certainly not by intention. Epistemological vertigo is always possible when controversial issues are raised. For this reason, the following things should be kept in mind.

Tough issues put Christian maturity to the test.

A married couple shared an experience they had had in a weekly home Bible study they were in before coming to our congregation. A man in the group spoke at length and with passion about what he believed to be the sins of abortion and homosexuality. They said they chose to remain silent even though their beliefs on these two issues were very different from his. When asked why they didn't speak up, they responded, "It just didn't feel safe to do so."

Something is wrong at the heart of the Christian community when a Bible study group is not a safe place for people to share openly and honestly what they believe. Yet this couple's experience is all too common in Christian gatherings. People refuse to discuss their deepest-held beliefs for fear of being attacked or condemned. It should not be this way. It strikes me as quite inconsistent with the Jesus we find in the gospels for churches not to foster an open and free dialogue. That they do not is indicative of the degree to which all of us stand in need of prayer for continued growth in both grace and humility.

It takes spiritual maturity to disagree with someone respectfully, especially when convictions run deep. The only way to have such maturity is to follow the words of the apostle Paul (who had his own differences with Peter) when he wrote, "Let the same mind be in you that was in Christ Jesus" (Phil. 2:5). In practical terms this points to a basic truth Dwight and Linda Vogel have expressed so well:

> To be one with Christ means that we are called to be one with all Christians. And whenever we are tempted to draw lines which make us insiders and place others who claim Christ's name on the outside, we run the risk of receiving the same reprimand Jesus gave to the Pharisees of his day.[2]

The issues below are tough ones that test our capacity to think with the mind of Christ. They will reveal how deep our commitment is to the bond of Christian fellowship we share in a community that includes diverse perspectives. Some Christians believe such matters should be avoided, but that is only to institutionalize attitudes that prevent maturity of heart and mind or becoming an ambassador of reconciliation (2 Cor. 5:20). The basic challenge is to be able to think about controversial issues and also remain Christian in attitudes and actions.

None of us is God.

One step in this direction is to remember that there is only one God and that none of us is a candidate. Nothing makes for a poor witness to the gospel of Jesus Christ more than self-righteousness, yet that characteristic often appears to be ubiquitous in the Christian community. How ironic that Christians who are quite ready to name the sins of others are not able to see this one in themselves. Jesus once spoke about the danger of this tendency:

> "Why do you see the speck in your neighbor's eye, but do not notice the log in your own eye? Or how can you say to your neighbor, 'Let me take the speck out of your eye,' while the log is in your own eye? You hypocrite, first take the log out of your own eye, and then you will see clearly to take the speck out of your neighbor's eye." (Mt. 7:3–5)

Liberals see the speck in the eye of conservatives; conservatives see it in liberals; and fundamentalists see it in both, but seldom do any of the three see it in themselves. That is why it is so dangerous. Self-righteousness has led Christians to commit some of the worst atrocities in history. The Crusades, the Spanish Inquisition, the Holocaust, the annihilation of Native American land and culture, the support of slavery, and the toleration of poverty in a nation of immense wealth all come to mind. Self-righteousness leads to horrible things being done in the name of Jesus. Making matters worse is the hypocrisy that accompanies it. One always exists with the other. Together they undermine the integrity of Christian faith and witness.

Important issues exist within polarities because that is the nature of human perception. This is what we said in the section on the Bible. Tough issues challenge us precisely because we are forced to discern truth within the limitations of fallibility. Thus, the more important the issue, the more controversy there is around it. Genuine and respectful discussion and dialogue are possible only when humility, rather than self-righteousness, characterizes the spirit of those participating. The basis for such humility is the confession that we are not God, and, therefore, know truth only within human limitations.

Knowing what's right is sometimes as clear as mud.

"Clear ambiguity" is the place many of us find ourselves when it comes to controversial issues. This doesn't mean we are waffling or are afraid to say what we think. It simply means that the right thing to believe or do is not clear to us. We feel pulled in different directions emotionally and intellectually. Indeed, at times our heads and hearts seem to be moving in opposite directions. Many people are uncomfortable with ambiguity because of their need for order and their low tolerance for gray areas. Gray is the color of ambiguity, and it seldom makes for much order. Things weave back and forth as if one were in a maze, and clearness can be a long time in coming.

A presupposition basic to the positions offered below is that clear ambiguity is an acceptable state, because that is the way life is generally lived in the real world. Theories and principles can be clear, but living them hardly ever is. Recall the Ten Boom family in

Holland during World War II, who created a hiding place in their home for Jews, refusing to reveal the secret when questioned by the Nazis. I think of Nelson Mandela and his colleagues, who often lied to protect themselves or someone else from the injustice of apartheid. The commandment says not to lie, but lying can become a necessary tool for protecting innocent people from evil. Clear ambiguity is sometimes the best a principled person can do under difficult circumstances. Any belief system that does not make room for it will ultimately fall under its own weight.

Controversial issues that divide Christians require humility and at times clear ambiguity as we try to find our way through them. Both are rooted in the fact that Jesus said nothing in any direct way about most of the issues we confront today. On many of the matters we shall discuss the best we can do is to draw inferences from what he said, a point we will emphasize again and again because all inferences are subject to human weaknesses and flaws. No inference can be equated with the command of God without being dishonest. There are, to be sure, established moral imperatives about which all reasonable Christians can agree. Racial equality and racial justice are notable examples. So is treating all persons and cultural traditions with respect and dignity. The sanctity of life and the rejection of social and economic systems that undermine it is another. So is the need for personal and corporate integrity. Others, of course, could be cited. Our point is that even where there is general agreement on moral obligations, conclusions about what it means to put them into practice can be perplexing. Besides that, none of us lives up to our best intentions even when we know what to do or not do. As a friend recently reminded me, the Jews were very good at making laws; they just weren't very good at keeping them. The same can be said of Christians. It is far easier for us to say what we believe is morally right than to do it. This is the reason we are saved by grace rather than by merit.

But the rejoinder to this point of view is that it makes it impossible for Christians to say anything definitive about moral issues. That is not a bad place to be for Christians who are often too quick to speak and very wrong when they do. Yet the solution to moralism is hardly to be found in extreme individualism that rejects communal standards altogether. But there is an alternative to both:

spiritual guidance rather than moral imperatives. Silence on important issues is not a meaningful witness to the gospel, but neither is speaking in absolutes. The challenge is to offer the best faith perspective we can discern on issues without claiming to know truth infallibly. This is a reasonable perspective that allows us to have a voice that speaks with conviction and humility, a voice that non-Christians may be able to hear. Closed-mindedness will never produce greater obedience to Christian teachings; rather, it nurtures deviance and resentment. Spiritual guidance without imperatives *invites* rather than demands affirmation of the gospel.

The issues discussed below will be approached from this perspective. The sequence is intentional. The first three are primarily matters of conscience, while the second three have civil law implications.

Premarital sex is about more than yes or no.

The dominant culture today trivializes sex by using it as a marketing tool for anything and everything. It's everywhere, from television to magazines to movies to bigger-than-life billboards along the highway. It's no secret. Sex sells. Is it any wonder that kids are having kids? Yet some Christians still mention the word *sex* in hushed tones. They are afraid to talk about it. But the cat is out of the bag, so to speak. Everybody talks about sex. Christians can too.

The first thing we can do is to ask what the Bible says about premarital sex. The truth is, it says very little. The apostle Paul speaks about it, but in all candor his is a rather negative view of both sex and marriage:

> To the unmarried and the widows I say that it is well for them to remain unmarried as I am. But if they are not practicing self-control, they should marry. For it is better to marry than to be aflame with passion. (1 Cor. 7:8–9)

In this text Paul's position is that failure to practice sexual abstinence is a justifiable basis for marriage, advice no parent or church would give to singles today. Worse, it undercuts the argument that sex is more than physical union and that marriage is more than sex. Christians believe that both sex and marriage are sacred unions born of spiritual maturity, but that is hardly what

Paul suggests here. We can be thankful that Paul admits that his views on premarital sex are his own and not necessarily those of Jesus: "Now concerning virgins, I have no command of the Lord, but I give my opinion as one who by the Lord's mercy is trustworthy" (1 Cor. 7:25). The Contemporary English Version translates the verse this way: "I don't know of anything that the Lord said about people who have never been married. But I will tell you what I think." The Greek word sometimes associated with premarital sex, *fornication,* does not actually mean that. It refers, rather, to adultery, incest, prostitution, and figuratively to idolatry. Any connection between fornication and premarital sex is a culturally conditioned understanding of the term. Further, while Torah law speaks of marriage, it does not offer any specific rules regarding premarital sex. No doubt part of the reason for this is the fact that marriage occurred at a very early age in biblical times. To the extent that sex before marriage was an issue, it had to do with rape, incest, adultery, or prostitution, as the word *fornication* indicates.

The conclusion one has to reach is that the Bible leaves us without much direct moral guidance about premarital sex. The most we can discern from scripture is that sex is a powerful drive that can lead people into actions that have tragic consequences. This is old news, of course. But such dire consequences do not resolve the issue for unmarried Christian couples deeply in love who are not sure about what is right and wrong as they struggle to maintain control of their sexual drives. Although churches generally do not talk openly about sex, the message is clear nonetheless. Sex is reserved for marriage. What is not very clear is why. For young adult Christians premarital sex can never be casual, but neither can they agree that it is a mortal sin or that abstinence as a commandment is justified by an honest reading of the Bible.

Under the circumstances, it may be that the best the Christian community can do is to provide thoughtful guidance about sex before marriage that balances the church's traditional perspective with commonsense wisdom that applies to any age. To this end, then, the first thing that makes sense to believe is that *sexual abstinence before marriage is a wise and enduring moral standard every Christian can trust to be the best alternative to sexual behavior outside of marriage.* A standard is not a commandment; it is a norm.

This is how, as open-minded Christians, we can think about abstinence. Rather than viewing it as a rule to be enforced, think of it as a standard by which Christian singles can measure other perspectives. Obviously, it is the safest behavior in terms of the medical and emotional consequences of premarital sex. But it is also consistent with the biblical assumption that marriage is the foundation for the family and that the family is the anchor for society in general. Issues related to sex, such as adultery, were treated within the context of this presumption of marriage. In addition, abstinence before marriage goes beyond commandment in inviting men and women to view human sexuality as a spiritual discipline that leads to fulfillment and wholeness. This point of view is what lies behind the concept of priestly celibacy. But it is a practice open to all Christians at various stages of their journey who would choose it as a means of spiritual growth and development. It is an alternative you can believe to be not only right but reasonable. In short, it can be done, and when it is, it often brings a fresh sense of spiritual vitality and maturity.

An important distinction related to this subject is the fact that sex before marriage is not the same issue for young adults as it is for teenagers. The reason is a simple one: personal maturity. While there are quite mature teenagers and equally immature young adults, it remains wise counsel to teens to say that *sex before marriage is always dangerous and always wrong*. It is dangerous because they do not possess the emotional maturity to understand the potential it has for damaging their lives and those of others. It outdistances their level of maturity in coping with the full impact of their actions. Indeed, while there is a general consensus among adults that abstinence allows for no form of intercourse, surveys among teens tell us they are very confused on this matter. A study of teenage boys between the ages of fifteen and nineteen, for example, found that many of them considered oral and anal sex consistent with abstinence.[3] A similar survey of Midwestern teens between the ages of twelve and seventeen who had gone through an abstinence educational program revealed that they considered vaginal intercourse the only violation of abstinence.[4] Clearly many teens do not even understand what sexual abstinence means, making their need for it all the more urgent.

But, of course, telling teenagers to abstain does not make it happen. This means parents face the daunting challenge of establishing trust and communication with their children in the hope of instilling a good measure of education about the responsibilities that go with sexual relations and the dangers of premarital sex along with the reasons they hope their children will abstain from sexual activity at this time in their lives. Parents should talk to their children about human sexuality holistically, and within that context discuss the wisdom of abstinence and other appropriate sexual norms and behaviors. Children need parents to be in the sexual conversation. In turn, parents need churches to support them by talking openly to teens about sexual abstinence in youth groups and educational classes. Schools teach about sex because of the federal mandate regarding HIV/AIDS education, but they are not permitted to bring a spiritual perspective to the subject. Churches can and should. They can encourage parents not to surrender to their fears by providing their teens with condoms or birth control pills, thinking that is the only responsible way to protect teens from themselves. In reality this is giving up and giving in to what seems inevitable but isn't. There is nothing to make one believe that teens want parents to give up so easily. On the contrary, what they not only need but also show every indication of wanting is for parents to be buffers against their own wishes. To an amazing degree teens know when they need help in making it through these years. They will insist on making up their own minds, but they are not ready to have their parents always agree with them on the tough issues they face. Simply put, parents are the safety net teens need even when they push against it. Premarital sex is much like the use of drugs. It is dangerous and wrong for teens, and Christian parents can be confident they are doing right by their kids when they stand firm on this issue.

For young adult Christian singles the issue of premarital sex moves to a higher level. I define *adult* as beyond the high school years. Once teenagers leave high school, everything in their lives changes. In most respects society recognizes them as adults who must accept responsibility for themselves. It seems wise for the Christian community to do the same. Abstinence, of course, remains the standard for all single Christians. In addition, casual or recreational sex, that is, sex for the sake of the pleasure of sex, is an unacceptable standard. A foolish disregard of the seriousness of sexual intimacy can never be viewed either as good or even as a reflection of common sense. Sex is more than a moment of physical pleasure. Sex without respect for emotional and spiritual wholeness comes close to being an act of abuse, whether it is done to oneself or to another. It would fit into the category of illicit sex that Paul opposed in his first letter to the Corinthian Christians (1 Cor. 5:1–2). The caveat we would add to the apostle's counsel is that today we would not presume that sexual relations within marriage always meet this same standard, but in fact they should.

At the same time, it is important for the church to convey its trust of single adult Christians to make good decisions about sex that are consistent with their Christian commitment. It should trust that single adult Christians want to live by high moral standards and that they understand that the responsibility for deciding what is right and wrong is an awesome one, because the potential for making the wrong decision is always present. This trust puts the church in the position of offering spiritual counsel that has credibility beyond the exercise of authority. Part of that counsel can be that while there may not be a commandment against doing something, doing it may not be beneficial, something the apostle Paul wrote that actually is helpful regarding this issue (1 Cor. 6:12).

This is simply commonsense advice to single adult Christians as they struggle with the issue of sex before marriage. Moreover, one of the ways to determine what is beneficial is for both partners to know the long-term intentions of each other before any decision about sex is made. It is always important in serious relationships to know the degree of love and commitment each has for the other. Fears about marriage can often blur the nature of the relationship. But in a healthy relationship, couples enjoy open communication that allows them to explore whether or not there is reason to believe a foundation for a future together is being built. Love and commitment are essential for right sexual relations in all circumstances, including marriage. Couples who have clarified where their relationship stands in regard to both are likely to make a wise decision.

The irony of affirming abstinence within the context of no definitive biblical direction about sex before marriage is that the most holistic perspective on the subject might have come from the apostle Paul after all when he urged the Corinthian Christians to view their bodies as "a temple of the Holy Spirit," belonging to God and not just to them (1 Cor. 6:19–20). To follow this advice means all decisions about sex, before and within marriage, are guided by the desire to use our bodies in ways that are consistent with being God's temple. All those who have the emotional and spiritual maturity to do this can be trusted to make good decisions about their bodies.

One final word. In the end any Christian standard regarding premarital sex is itself accountable to the mercy of God's love. Grace always provides balance to obedience, lest standards become tyrannical.

Divorce is worse than you may think.

Early in ministry I spent hours of pastoral counseling time trying to help couples resolve problems that threatened their marriages. More times than not it didn't work. I remember thinking that two people who loved each other ought to be able to work things out, especially if they were Christians. Never once did it occur to me that my marriage would fail. Quite the opposite, in fact. It not only wouldn't happen. It couldn't happen. Not to me. How arrogantly wrong I was! It was the worst experience of my life. Every day I live with its consequences. There will never be a time when I will not feel the sense of failure I have about it. Time does heal wounds, but scars remain.

We live at a time when the family and family values have become mainstream issues, and for good reason. Four of every ten marriages end in divorce, a statistic of no small importance. All who have been through it know that the failure of a marriage is a devastating experience. They also know that a healthy marriage is essential to a healthy family. This is why the Christian community affirms both the sanctity of marriage and the tragedy of divorce. People who are divorced would agree with both. They would say that marriage is a sacred union, and they entered into it with that attitude. If anything, divorce heightens their commitment to the sanctity of marriage, with 81 percent saying they still believe marriage should be for life.[5]

That statistic may seem surprising, but no more so than the fact that conservative Christian views on divorce apparently do not translate into better marriages. Among Christians who call themselves "born again" 27 percent are divorced, a rate higher than the 23 percent for the general population. In 87 percent of these failed marriages, the divorce occurred after conversion, and of this number 30 percent involved fundamentalist Christians. But the most important finding may be that these people "feel their community of faith provides rejection rather than support and healing."[6] No clearer example of the validity of their resentment exists than the Roman Catholic practice of excluding divorced members from the sacrament of communion, especially in light of the dubious practice of annulment.

Most of us have known Catholic and Protestant Christians whose pain from divorce has been exacerbated by the church's response to them. A young man from an evangelical church was told by his pastor that he had to resign from his leadership position in the church after the pastor learned that the young man was separated from his wife. A friend who was an active Catholic from early childhood, who married in the church and took her children to Mass regularly, was told she could no longer receive communion after leaving a bad situation in her marriage. In another instance a young man serving in his first pastorate was asked by his lay leaders to resign when he informed them that he and his wife had separated but were still working to save the marriage. These are examples of numerous occasions when, instead of providing love and support for those who are experiencing the agony of a divorce, churches choose to shoot the wounded.

The justification, of course, is that divorce is a sin. If that is the case, and we shall look at this in a moment, there is no explanation as to what makes it a sin worse than any other or how exclusion and judgmentalism constitute an appropriate response to any sin. Worse, though, is the fact that uncaring attitudes and practices by Christians offer no reasonable alternative to leaving a bad marriage, even when a spouse and/or children are living in dangerously abusive circumstances. That, of course, is part of the problem. When Christians speak in moral imperatives, circumstances seem to make no difference. But even the words of Jesus do not support such rigidity.

> "It was also said, 'Whoever divorces his wife, let him give her a certificate of divorce.' But I say to you that anyone who divorces his wife, except on the ground of unchastity, causes her to commit adultery; and whoever marries a divorced woman commits adultery." (Mt. 5:31–32)

Some Pharisees came to him, and to test him they asked, "Is it lawful for a man to divorce his wife for any cause?" He answered, "Have you not read that the one who made them at the beginning 'made them male and female,' and said, 'For this reason a man shall leave his father and mother and be joined to his wife, and the two shall become one flesh'? So they are no longer two, but one flesh. Therefore what God has joined together, let no one separate." They said to him, "Why then did Moses command us to give a certificate of dismissal and to divorce her?" He said to them, "It was because you were so hard-hearted that Moses allowed you to divorce your wives, but from the beginning it was not so. And I say to you, whoever divorces his wife, except for unchastity, and marries another commits adultery." (Mt. 19:3–9)

Some Pharisees came, and to test him they asked, "Is it lawful for a man to divorce his wife?" He answered them, "What did Moses command you?" They said, "Moses allowed a man to write a certificate of dismissal and to divorce her." But Jesus said to them, "Because of your hardness of heart he wrote this commandment for you. But from the beginning of creation, 'God made them male and female.' 'For this reason a man shall leave his father and mother and be joined to his wife, and the two shall become one flesh.' So they are no longer two, but one flesh. Therefore what God has joined together, let no one separate." (Mk. 10:2–9)

In the first Matthew passage Jesus says that only adultery can be a justification for divorce. In doing so he not only lent support to the followers of the school of Shammai who viewed divorce in this way but also made a direct challenge to the prevailing attitudes about women. Torah permitted a man to divorce his wife on just about any grounds he might concoct. Women were property to be "thrown away," which is the literal meaning of the word *divorce*. The reason Jesus says divorce makes a woman a prostitute is because she had no other way to make a living once her husband threw her away. She couldn't go back to school for a degree. She couldn't resume the career in business or education she gave up to marry. But she could sell the only thing she had—herself. By limiting the grounds for divorce to adultery, he was narrowing the scope of male freedom to throw a wife away like an old piece of cloth. Any man who divorced for some other reason was not in fact free from his marriage obligations. Thus, if he married again, he was guilty of committing adultery himself, a sin punishable by death. In this way Jesus raised the stakes and called for men to act in a more just way toward women.

In the second Matthew text Jesus tells the Pharisees that the reason Torah allowed divorce at all was because of human sinfulness, but it was never the intention of God. Marriage was a holy union because God was joining two people together, a union not to be broken by human action. In this regard this text is more consistent with the gospel of Mark than the earlier one. In Mark, Jesus offers no basis for divorce. Luke follows Mark and says the same thing (Lk. 16:18). It is likely that Mark is the more accurate account of Jesus' words, but the real meaning of the text is not a new legalism—that is, no divorce on any grounds. When Jesus says that marriage reflects the intentions of God and divorce goes against it, he is establishing the standard or norm to be followed. Marriage is the will of God. Divorce is not. But this teaching becomes a new legalism when we push it into a commandment that declares Christians must remain married even under the worst possible circumstances. Richard Foster offers insight into this matter when he writes,

> Jesus was not trying to set down a legalistic set of rules to determine when a divorce was allowable...he was striking

at the spirit in which people live with each other. And so when we study Jesus' teaching on divorce…we are to see the heart of [his] teaching on human relationships within the context of first-century Palestine and seek to interpret those insights in the context of our world.[7]

Many Christians who think that Judaism is all about laws and commandments (this is not the case, of course) often turn the teachings of Jesus into precisely that. As a result the spirit of the law to which Jesus most often pointed is overshadowed. His words about divorce challenged prevailing attitudes about women being treated as property. To say that a woman (or man) must remain married under conditions in which she (or he) is being treated in just this way (as, for example, in a physically abusive situation) would violate and abrogate the very reason he said what he did. At the same time, the fact that the Jesus in the gospels of Matthew and Mark says different things about divorce is itself a word of caution about turning either text into legalism.

It is also quite telling that while Jesus spoke about the efficacy of marriage, he did not say what the Christian community should do about members who divorce. It seems unlikely that he thought the weaknesses of the flesh that made divorce a reality among Jews would not be present among his followers. Nor does anything else he said suggest that he would want divorced Christians purged from the church. What we are left with is the startling and awesome fact that *Jesus left the church with the responsibility of struggling with the appropriate attitude toward divorce.* The issue comes down to how the sanctity of marriage can remain the standard to follow while Christians go through divorce. The fact that Jesus doesn't tell us means we have to work this out on our own.

Yet he did provide some guidance we can trust. It is found in the example he set in how he responded to those whose sins were exposed. He forgave them. The last word in all his encounters with people was forgiveness. The last word in all his teachings is forgiveness. Here you have the answer to how Christians today can approach the issue of divorce. Based on the ministry of Jesus, if we are to err, it should be on the side of compassion and forgiveness. A tax collector is forgiven and made a disciple. A woman caught in adultery is forgiven and sent on her way. A wayward son is received back home. The gospel has standards, but the last word is always forgiveness.

Yet this word of forgiveness will not be heard if Christians speak against divorce as a moral imperative. Rather than a commandment forbidding it, more consistent with Jesus' total ministry would be the counsel that *under particular circumstances divorce is a justifiable decision that violates God's intention for marriage*. The question, of course, is, What circumstances? Adultery? Possibly, but not always. Abuse? Likely, but not necessarily. Irreconcilable differences? Unlikely, but possible. There is no proscriptive answer. You have no choice but to trust the integrity of people's assessments of the circumstances they face when making the decision to end a marriage. Limiting circumstances in advance leads to more problems than leaving the matter open-ended. Just as one cannot know how devastating divorce is unless one has gone through it, no one can judge the "rightness" of circumstances that would justify or nullify it except those who are living in them. This was never more apparent to me than the beautiful story of a clergy friend some years ago.

He spent many happy years married to a wonderful woman. Together they raised three children who had become outstanding young adults. But then they discovered she had Huntington's Disease, incurable, and worse, hereditary. For several years he cared for her while continuing in full-time ministry. Eventually she became bedfast and reached the point of being unable to respond in any way to her surroundings. It was during this time that he became reacquainted with a friend of years past. They fell in love. Both of them met with his children and with leaders in his church to ask their blessing on his petitioning the court for a divorce to marry his new love, and then both of them become the legal custodians of his sick wife for the remaining years of her life. The children and the church consented without hesitation. It was done, and this good man began a new life with a woman he loved dearly, all the while keeping faith with his commitment to care for his first wife until death parted them. Those of us who knew him rejoiced over his newfound happiness.

Circumstances must be the final arbiter in decisions about divorce, even as the standard of marriage for life is maintained. Another way of saying this is that in some instances divorce may be justified, even though it goes against God's will for marriage. In the real world of lived relationships, divorce may be the most reasonable resolution of a breached relationship that cannot be restored. Yet in itself it is an acknowledgment that a union intended for life has been broken, and everyone touched by it, especially children, have suffered damage. In the novel by Larry Watson entitled *Laura,* Robert Finley is telling his son Judge, the book's narrator, that he and his mother are divorcing. The conversation below picks up after Judge has asked where his father is planning to live.

> "I knew I wasn't doing this right...Judge, I'm sorry. I should have told you this right away. I'm going to stay in the house. At least for a while. Later we might try to sell it. But you and your mother and your sister are going to stay with Grandpa and Grandma Madden in Minnesota. I'm sorry I didn't tell you that right away."
>
> His apology didn't help. Immediately I began to cry, and the salty tears that ran down my cheeks mixed with the room's bitter smell of oranges, so that my tears seemed to turn to acid. I had known, I thought, everything; and now this, this surprise, this trick that showed me how quickly the world could cave in and how I could not prevent it. I cried because I would be leaving my friends, my school, my house, because I would never see them again, because I would never see Laura again. I was a child, and any adult of any size could pick me up and carry me out of my own life.
>
> My father dropped to his knees beside my chair. He put his hands on my ribs and shook me gently, lovingly, back and forth as if I were a baby that needed to be jollied from his tears. "Don't, Judge, please don't. Oh, Jesus, don't. This is hard enough."
>
> And then he started crying too, his own tears brimming over and streaking down his cheeks like raindrops running down a windowpane. And just as the rain distorts the view through the window glass, so was my father's face contorted by his crying. He put his arms around me, bumping his hand hard against the back of the chair. He let his head fall

forward into my lap, so I could no longer see his misshapen face; but from the way his back bounced, as though he had hiccups, I could tell his sobs continued. I patted the back of his head, right where his thinning hair let the skin show through. It was the first and last time I saw my father cry.[8]

Children of broken marriages adjust, but not without struggle and sometimes enduring confusion and pain. In-laws and grandparents feel the agony of being torn between two loves. And both partners in a divorce carry a sense of failure.

This is why compassion in the Christian community is so important. The sense of brokenness caused by divorce begs for an experience of healing and forgiveness at some level. For some this need is satisfied through resolution of anger or the overcoming of feelings of failure, betrayal, or rejection. In my own experience it came through a prayerful recognition that for me divorce was a justifiable sin. In that moment my mind and heart opened to God's forgiveness, and I experienced release from both guilt and shame. At the same time the community of faith where I was serving played a crucial role. I resigned once it was clear to me that my marriage was failing. I could accept others in ministry being divorced, but I was too proud to accept it for myself. That church's lay leaders were wiser than their pastor. They said no, suggesting I take some sabbatical time before making any permanent decision, and then assured me that there was still a place for me in the ministry we shared. I followed their counsel, which gave me a chance to distance myself, in part, from the struggle between ministry demands and personal pain. In the end I came to trust their wisdom, and that is why I am still in ministry today.

The church can help people of divorce to experience healing and forgiveness, if it has the spirit and will. Such a ministry of reconciliation is closer to the heart of Jesus than condemnation and rejection and does not conflict with affirming both the sanctity of marriage and the tragedy of divorce.

Homosexuality is about more than sex.

Nothing creates epistemological vertigo among Christians more than opposing views on homosexuality. As the Reverend Peter Gomes, Harvard chaplain, states it:

Among religious people who wish to take the Bible
seriously there is no more vexed topic today than that of
homosexuality…We have a contemporary, existential,
deeply felt struggle that shows no sign of going away, that
grows increasingly less civil, and upon which everyone has
an opinion and a text upon which to base it.[9]

When it comes to homosexuality, Christians often do not
understand how those who disagree with them can be so wrong.
Sides in this debate will talk past one another, impatient with the
"closed-mindedness" of the other. The need is to shift the debate to
a different level. The goal here is to be able to discuss homosexuality
in a way that advances both reconciliation and justice. It is a
daunting challenge.

There are three primary perspectives among Christians about
homosexuality. The first was clearly articulated by a Presbyterian
minister quoted in the local paper in response to his denomination's
decision to put to a vote in all its presbyteries its ban on accepting
noncelibate homosexuals into ministry. "I believe God loves all
people," said the Reverend Gary Le Tourneau, "but I do believe that
homosexual behavior is a sin and I agree with the church's stance
that homosexual practice is not God's will for humanity."[10]

This position is not without biblical foundation. In Leviticus
18:22 we find these words: "You shall not lie with a male as with a
woman; it is an abomination." The word *abomination* literally
means "disgusting" and carries the connotation of idolatry. Two
chapters later the command is elevated to grounds for one's being
put to death: "If a man lies with a male as with a woman, both of
them have committed an abomination; they shall be put to death;
their blood is upon them" (20:13). In the New Testament, Paul
addresses the issue this way:

> For the wrath of God is revealed from heaven against all
> ungodliness and wickedness of those who by their
> wickedness suppress the truth…For this reason God gave
> them up to degrading passions. Their women exchanged
> natural intercourse for unnatural, and in the same way also
> the men, giving up natural intercourse with women, were
> consumed with passion for one another. Men committed

shameless acts with men and received in their own persons the due penalty for their error. (Rom. 1:18, 26–27)

Paul also lists homosexuality as one of the several vices or violations of the law that exclude a person from participation in the kingdom of God in 1 Corinthians 6:9–10: "Do you not know that wrongdoers will not inherit the kingdom of God? Do not be deceived! Fornicators, idolaters, adulterers, male prostitutes, sodomites, thieves, the greedy, drunkards, revilers, robbers—none of these will inherit the kingdom of God," and in 1 Timothy 1:9–11:

> This means understanding that the law is laid down not for the innocent but for the lawless and disobedient, for the godless and sinful, for the unholy and profane, for those who kill their father or mother, for murderers, fornicators, sodomites, slave traders, liars, perjurers, and whatever else is contrary to the sound teaching that conforms to the glorious gospel of the blessed God, which he entrusted to me.

Those who share LeTourneau's perspective believe these texts state unequivocally that homosexual behavior is unacceptable to God, and, therefore, unacceptable to the church.

The second dominant perspective challenges this conclusion. Its advocates may (or may not) accept that these texts speak against homosexuality, but in any case they go on to argue that they are no different from other culturally conditioned texts such as those that give tacit or explicit approval of slavery or the resistance to women in ministry. Thus, they should be no more binding on church practices than those already rejected. As the Reverend Kim Smith King stated at the time of the Presbyterian vote, "From my perspective, we have reformed our thinking about divorce, slavery, women in ministry, and now we need to recognize the need to reform our thinking about sexuality."[11]

A third perspective—often, I might add, heard among laity—stands somewhere between these two extremes. On the surface it accepts the belief that homosexual behavior is sinful, but it is quick to add that it is no worse than other sin and should not be singled out. Those who take this view may not advocate accepting noncelibate homosexuals into church leadership, as Smith King urges, but neither are they ready to exclude them altogether, as LeTourneau wants to do. They sense that homosexuality is not only a theological issue, or solely a matter of morality or justice, but is an ecclesiological issue that touches the tension between communal integrity and the oneness of the church. They also understand that insistence with either of the two extreme positions without regard for this oneness undercuts the cause of Christ to the world.

This third view is most unlike the first two because it is less rigid, fraught with ambiguity, and far from fixed. Yet for these same reasons it offers a point of departure in finding a place to stand for Christians who want to be faithful to the gospel and at the same time open-minded in dealing with homosexuality. The need is to go further than those who believe homosexual behavior is sinful have been willing to go, but not as far as those who advocate full acceptance of openly homosexual persons into ministry. This point of view, let us call it the ambiguous view, has genuine possibilities in this regard.

For one thing it acknowledges what neither extreme is willing to admit. All views about homosexuality are to a significant degree the result of cultural conditioning. This is true whether it is found in the Bible or among today's church. I grew up during a time when homosexuality was considered a perversion; it was labeled a mental disorder by the American Psychiatric Association until the late 1970s. Homosexuals were thought to be social deviants who preyed on children. In high school there was a student rumored to be gay who was subjected to all manner of ridicule. This was a time when homosexual entertainers did not risk coming out. My favorite pop singer was Johnny Mathis. I remember the disappointment I felt when I found out he was gay, as if I had been personally betrayed by him. That was the world in which my attitudes were shaped and molded.

My children grew up in a very different world. One of our daughters was a drama major in college. Virtually every male friend she had was gay. Through the years some of them have remained close friends. Two who are in a partnership with each other not only attended but participated in her wedding. It never occurred to her not to accept these friends for who they are, a point of view far removed from the one instilled in me. This simple difference underscores the fact that the way we think about every issue, and this one in particular, is rooted in the cultural conditioning we experience early in life. This does not mean that attitudes have to be fixed, only that all of us begin with certain realities born of external influences we might not have chosen but by which we were influenced and shaped. To admit this helps to bring the issue down to a human level and exposes the potential for fears, prejudice, and misunderstanding lying at the core of what we believe and think.

This is no small matter, a point a recent letter in the local paper from a mother whose son is gay poignantly makes:

> My [now] 14 year old son is gay…[he] has been called a girl, made fun of, and ostracized most of his life…boys ask him to prove he's really a boy. They threaten to staple his tongue to his chin. In private the straight boys flirt with him and touch him and try to get him to teach them…He changes for gym class in the office because the other boys stare at him, waiting to see if he can prove he's a boy or whether he makes a move where they can accuse him of looking at them. He spent lunchtime in the school library because no one would let him sit with them. He even got asked to move when he sat at a table alone.

> When my son at the age of 12 told me…that he was gay, while he was crying and wishing he was dead, I didn't know what to do. I wanted to stop the pain. I wanted to grab all the people in the world who have hurt him personally or through articles…and drag them into my house and show them the results of their words and actions. Instead I got my son antidepressants and therapy once a week.

Then she wrote:

> My son and I don't go to church anymore. Even though not all churches preach hatred, the institution has come to represent pain. God's name has been used so much to frighten and hurt people. So I keep asking God to please

help people...see and understand what they are doing to God's children so all this can please stop.[12]

But people—including Christians—often don't see or understand. In a conversation with teenagers in our church, they described a sandlot football game they play called "Smear the Queer." Someone throws up the ball, and when one person catches it, the others yell, "Smear the queer." I asked them why as Christian teenagers they participated in it. They replied, "It's just a game."

But, of course, it isn't. The U.S. Constitution declares, "No religious test shall ever be required as a qualification to any office or public trust under the United States" (Article 6, paragraph 3). Yet open discrimination at the highest levels of government is common and supported by Christian fundamentalists. In 1997 a handful of Republican senators blocked the 1997 nomination of James Hormel, an openly gay man, to be Ambassador to Luxembourg, their disclaimer that it was not because he was homosexual notwithstanding. Worse, though, are the hate crimes that gay-bashing invites. On October 8, 1998, Matthew Shepard, a twenty-two-year-old openly gay student at the University of Wyoming, was brutally beaten by gay-bashers in Laramie, Wyoming. He was found dead tied to a fence. In researching for her book *The Drowning of Stephan Jones,* the true story of a young gay man who was tossed from a bridge to his death by gay-bashers, author Bette Greene found little remorse among the more than four hundred young men in jail for a variety of hate crimes against gays. Worse, a number of them said they felt their religious tradition justified their actions against homosexuals.[13]

Most Christians will, of course, see open gay-bashing as repugnant, yet they are sometimes unwilling to consider how their attitudes might indirectly encourage such things. But those who are ambiguous do see the connection. Unclear about what is morally right in regard to homosexuality and disgusted by actions they know are morally wrong, they refuse to accept attitudes that may in fact encourage gay-bashing, if only by remaining silent in the face of them.

A second reason the ambiguous position offers a path to open-minded faith is that it reflects the fact that Jesus did not address the subject of homosexuality in a direct way, a good reason in itself to be puzzled by some Christians' making it the primary issue for the church today. Indeed, the fact that Jesus made justice for the poor the primary example of kingdom living (Mt. 25:31–45; Lk. 16:19–31) makes ambiguity about homosexuality all the more understandable. The best one can do regarding this subject when it comes to the gospels is to make inferences, a fact that should challenge any view that is expressed in absolutes. The truth is, discernment is the only available path for finding our way through this controversy, and discernment always involves walking by faith (2 Cor. 5:7). The gospels' silence about homosexuality is an implicit argument against making acceptance of homosexual behavior a litmus test for justice or opposing it a litmus test for Christian morality.

Moreover, the few biblical texts that speak about homosexuality do not censure it as a sin greater than any other. From a biblical perspective sin is sin; therefore, forgiveness is forgiveness. All receive it because all need it. Were forgiveness a reward for personal goodness, no one would receive it: "But God proves his love for us in that while we still were sinners Christ died for us" (Rom. 5:8). Forgiveness is an extension of divine grace. It is a gift God chooses as the means of overcoming the effects of human sin, and all people share in the benefits of this mercy. Repentance positions one to experience what God has made possible, but it does not create that possibility. The heart of God does, and it goes out to everyone.

Should this sound as if people can do anything and still be forgiven, it is not a new concern. Paul confronted it when he wrote,

> What then are we to say? Should we continue in sin in order that grace may abound? By no means! How can we who died to sin go on living in it? Do you not know that all of us who have been baptized into Christ Jesus were baptized into his death? Therefore we have been buried with him by baptism into death, so that, just as Christ was raised from the dead by the glory of the Father, so we too might walk in newness of life." (Rom. 6:1–4)

Paul believed that the awareness of forgiveness made people more aware of the need for it rather than leading them into irresponsible behavior.

The point all of this makes in regard to homosexuality being a sin is this: If it is, then those guilty of it are the recipients of forgiveness because of divine grace, as all other sinners are. Homosexuals are children of God who struggle with sin as do heterosexuals, affirming the bond of common humanity all Christians—and all persons—share. No person stands above another. Thus, the basis for loving one another is not moral purity or righteous living, but salvation through grace that bespeaks a divine forgiveness no one deserves but all are given. In short, we love because God first loved us (1 Jn. 4:19).

Herein lies the hope for an attitude that balances moral convictions with justice-seeking and promotes reconciliation rather than hostility among Christians. Once homosexual persons are understood as people of faith who share a common humanity with heterosexuals, the issue shifts to a different level, to the question of willful sin. To be guilty of willful sin requires one to be conscious of the wrong being committed. But homosexual persons do not understand their behavior as sinful, because it is, they believe, part of who God made them to be. This means that the real issue is whether or not Christians who believe that homosexuality is a sin can trust the sincerity of homosexual persons who believe that they were born to be who they are. This is not about agreeing with them, but about believing the sincerity of their convictions. If this step can be taken, then *willful* sin is no longer an issue.

Yet there are some who want to respond to this position by saying that pedophiles sometimes claim they commit such acts for the same reason—that they were made the way they are. The illogic of such a point of view seems so obvious that it is not easy to take it seriously. Homosexual behavior is certainly not as criminal or injurious or heinous as pedophilia (or any other criminal behavior) clearly is, and to compare the two is itself an act of injustice of the worst kind. Moreover, while no research would support the notion that pedophilia is genetically determined, there is growing evidence that homosexuality is. Only those who do not want to know the truth can dismiss the preliminary research findings in this area.[14]

So we come back to the basic affirmation we have been making. All Christians share a common humanity and also a common need for forgiveness. Thus, believing that heterosexuality is intrinsically morally right and homosexuality is intrinsically morally wrong is a stroke too broad in its sweep, because it fails to take into account the reality that all people are sinful and that no one and no group stands above others in the eyes of God. As the apostle Paul stated, "For there is no distinction, since all have sinned and fall short of the glory of God" (Rom. 3:22b–23). In light of what we have said, those Christians who want to exclude homosexuals from church leadership face the dilemma of having to choose between competing values—their moral convictions and the gospel's call to love one another. The phrase "love the sinner, hate the sin" rings hollow in light of their own propensity for sin. If God loves the sinner but hates the sin, then God must love everyone and also hate what everyone does precisely because sin is the human condition. Thus, if homosexual behavior is sinful, and if on biblical grounds it cannot be singled out as any worse than any other sin, then the sinfulness of those who "hate the sin but love the sinner" becomes all the more perplexing in that they are but one step away from self-condemnation. The only way to make one sin worse than another is to assume that one's own sins are always less egregious than the one being condemned. That is a slippery slope indeed.

If being a true follower of Jesus requires moral purity, none of us should consider ourselves his disciples. If, on the other hand, the biblical message is clear in saying, as I submit it is, that belonging to him means seeking to please him in spite of our sinfulness, then all who seek to live this way are his true followers. But living this out in Christian community is far from simple or easy. Concern for the oneness of the church previously mentioned immediately comes to the forefront. Here's the reality. At the present moment the majority of Christians who make up mainline congregations have yet to be persuaded that sexual orientation is irrelevant for discipleship and ministry. They may accept it as a reality, and perhaps even that it is genetically determined, but they are not ready to affirm it as natural or normative. This means that imposing any view is likely to result in a splintering of mainline churches the likes of which we have never seen. While some congregations and denominations have voted to become what is called "open and affirming" in their acceptance of homosexual persons into the ranks of both membership and ministry, these remain the exception rather than the rule. Moreover, in most instances the battle they fought to win this victory was not without major casualties.

Here's the second reality. In a divided community those who advocate full acceptance of openly homosexual persons into ministry also face the dilemma of choosing between competing values—justice and unity. They have generally been those who have prayed and worked for the fulfillment of Jesus' prayer that his church be one (Jn. 17:1–26). Yet their convictions about homosexuality are a direct threat to this hope. Some may believe that a lack of unity is the price that must be paid for justice. So said the Reverend Kim Smith King, "We can't deny justice for the sake of peace." That is one view, fraught with inconsistencies as it may be. But another suggests that reconciliation can be a guide as Christians live their way into oneness in this matter. If peace needs justice to be biblical peace, it seems equally compelling that biblical justice has no less need for reconciliation. If so, then instead of disunity and schism being the price Christians must pay for justice regarding homosexuality, *working for consensus can be seen as an incredible opportunity for making a winsome witness to both justice and unity.*

This is not a position without precedence. New Testament scholar Father Raymond Brown took such a position concerning women priests. Believing that it would take at least two more popes before the church would seriously consider it, he said without hesitation that for the sake of the unity of the Roman church he accepted this reality. Mainline Protestant Christians would do well to have a similar concern for balancing justice and unity as we confront homosexuality.

Open-minded Christians can remain faithful to the gospel *and* admit to ambiguity on this issue. But that does not prevent us from advocating some practical steps that can enhance the prospects for reconciliation. One is the immediate acceptance into ministry of openly homosexual persons who are willing to remain celibate. Of one thing all Christians can be sure: There are homosexual persons doing effective ministry. Some are open while others remain in the closet, but in all instances ministry is taking place. Christian songs written by a gay man are being used regularly within fundamentalist circles. Without knowing it church members are being helped through personal crises by their homosexual pastors. The reality is that in terms of clergy leadership, the issue does not turn on whether or not homosexual persons can do effective ministry. They clearly do. The controversy revolves around allowing them to do so once they are out in the open.

Celibacy is one step toward this possibility, a position already accepted in the Roman Catholic Church. Celibacy *as a first step* is a practical way to move toward consensus without forcing it, thus serving as an important move toward reconciliation. Even more important, it introduces the human element into the situation, a factor often missing in debates on this issue, as the paths of homosexual clergy and those who in principle resist their serving in ministry cross. This meeting of persons will increase the chance for dialogue and even for moments of shared worship and prayer that may result in a level of understanding that will have the power to move them from tightly held positions to tightly clasping hands. But compromise on both sides will be needed. Those who believe that homosexuality is a sin must accept celibate homosexual persons into ministry. Those who are homosexual must live a celibate life, even though it is a double standard. This is a step that goes further than the former group has been willing to go, but doesn't go as far as the latter wants. However, it does open the door to further understanding and growth.

The road to open-mindedness offered above will not, of course, satisfy Christians whose views on this issue are fixed. But if history is any guide, we can be sure that the church's future does not lie in the extremes of any human perspective. That is because it is God's future that all Christians are called to seek, not their own, requiring a trust that God will shape the future and make the divine will known as God determines our readiness for it. Trusting this to be the case has been a path the people of God have had to travel since the beginning. But we believe in a God who can make a way when there doesn't seem to be one. That is the prayer all of us can pray.

But it will also take the best possible leadership within mainline churches. For this reason John Gardner's assessment of the need for leadership, though directed toward the power of special interest groups destroying the fabric of American social cohesiveness, speaks directly to the church. "Unfortunately," he says, "all too rarely have any of the special interests shown the slightest concern for the health of the political process." Yet the reality, he adds, is that "we cannot afford to continue our neglect of commonweal priorities."[15] Gardner, not one who could be accused of conservative views, challenges the dominance of political correctness within American society that has elevated rights above responsibility and labeled opposing views as discriminatory, in the process ignoring the reality that "everyone had better be partly responsible for the good of the whole."[16] But that takes leadership, Gardner says. Thus, the nation needs leaders in all aspects of society who are willing to "address themselves to community issues."[17]

So do mainline churches. We need leaders who see this difficult time as a special opportunity to witness to faith, justice, and reconciliation as equal concerns as we face the issue of homosexuality. They can do this by promoting consensus as the complementary process to discernment. Consensus is hardly passive. It requires clearness of motivation to ensure that what is being sought is God's will rather than personal victory. It relies on listening for decisions instead of simply making them. And it asks of everyone a high level of spiritual maturity. When the will of the majority becomes evident, those in the minority must honor that by stepping aside and allowing the sense of the group to move forward. They also need to work for the group's success even though they did not support the decision.

Leadership of this kind, however, will probably have to swim against the tide. Gardner says that groups want to win, not work with those outside their circle, which is why "a high proportion of leaders in all segments of our society today...are rewarded for single-minded pursuit of the interests of their group. They are rewarded for doing battle, not for compromising."[18] He suggests that a higher standard would be to reward them for accepting a larger responsibility in reaching beyond their own group without forgetting the goals of their own group."[19]

No better challenge can be given to church leaders and to all Christians as the church confronts the perplexing and vexing issue of homosexuality. The gospel calls on every Christian to consider the good of the whole regardless of the issue. In today's environment we seem to have forgotten Jesus' admonition that a house divided against itself cannot stand (Mk. 3:25). By intention, intuition, or the press of circumstances, those who find themselves on the ambiguous side of homosexuality are by example the hope for the mainline church. Neither extreme offers much more than polarization and eventual division. Those who stand in between are there only because a way marked by both reconciliation and unity has yet to be discerned. In the meantime they inch forward, taking those steps that they discern to be reasonable and that express trust that God is ahead of them and will show them the way.

Abortion is about more than being pro-life or pro-choice.

The two most often mentioned positions on abortion are pro-life and pro-choice. Essentially, being pro-life means being against abortions under any circumstances. The fullest expression of this viewpoint would be a return to the days before *Roe* v. *Wade* when abortion was illegal. Pro-choice, on the other hand, supports the 1972 Supreme Court ruling and resists any effort to restrict it. It holds that a woman's body is hers to do with as she chooses, and no one, especially men, should have the right to tell her otherwise.

Statistical data on abortion since legalization provide some indication of the impact it has had on American society. Two years after *Roe* v. *Wade* there were slightly fewer than a million abortions. The largest number occurred in 1990, with more than 1,600,000 abortions performed, but in the years since there has been a slow but consistent decline. In 1996 (the last year for which figures are presently available) there were 300,000 fewer abortions. The reason for this decline is unclear, but some observers believe it is due to family planning education.[20]

The abortion debate among Christians usually revolves around biblical texts that are used to prove or disprove points made by opposing sides. But can we get beyond "proof texting" to a careful examination of biblical texts that as much as possible resists one's agenda, thus predetermining the outcome? A series of articles on the Internet by B. A. Robinson of the Ontario Consultants on Religious Tolerance offers such a study. His work includes a detailed examination of the most-often-cited biblical texts in the abortion debate, extrabiblical Jewish and Christian sources, historical reviews of church tradition in such forms as papal decrees, and references to Roman and Greek sources that also address the subject. His research led him to conclude:

> Within Christianity, Judaism, Humanism and other religions and ethical systems, the morality of abortion hinges on what one believes about when life begins. There is a general consensus in North America that when the fetus becomes a human person, then abortions should be severely limited. Most would confine abortions at that stage to situations that threaten the life of the pregnant woman; a very few would eliminate access to abortions totally. The problem that generates the controversy centers on the question, "When does life actually begin?" This is the dilemma.[21]

Robinson's study of Old Testament material shows that in Hebrew thinking the concept of a "disembodied soul" is absent. When scripture says God made Adam's body out of the dust of the earth and he *became a living soul* only after God *"breathed into his nostrils the breath of life,"* this text is mostly interpreted to say that Adam's personhood started when he took his first breath. Robinson goes on to note that the most important word in the Hebrew Scriptures used to describe a person is *nephesh*, appearing some 755 times in the Old Testament. It is translated as "living soul" in the Genesis 2 passage. He cites Jewish scholar H. W. Wolff, who says that the word's root means "to breathe" and that during Old Testament times, *"Living creatures are in this way exactly defined in Hebrew as creatures that breathe."*[22]

The Talmud, the book of discussions and analysis of Jewish law and how it is applied in everyday life, also contains this view of when life begins. Specifically, it says that if the fetus is born normally, life begins when its forehead has left the birth canal. If the fetus is born feet-first, it happens when more than half of its body has been delivered. A newborn becomes human after it starts breathing; a fetus is only potentially human.

It is not surprising, then, that Conservative, Reform, and Reconstructionist Jews today support abortion rights. Some Orthodox Jews do with limitations, such as when the life of the mother is at risk. But it is without question that in Hebrew thinking during biblical times life was understood to begin at birth. Thus, citing the seventh commandment of the Decalogue, "You shall not murder," as an example of the Bible's condemning abortion is not justified by the text itself. The word is *murder*, not just *kill* (the Hebrew words are very different), and murder in ancient Israel involved premeditation in taking the life of a living person outside the womb.

The New Testament leaves us with even less to work with in regard to this issue.

Some Christians want to interpret Luke 1:41 as "the baby John moved inside Elizabeth when Mary the mother of Jesus greeted her when both were pregnant," but doing so is obviously an inference. The Didache, or "The Teaching of the Apostles," an important document of the early Christian church written by an unknown author, does speak against abortion. Section 2.2 reads: "Thou shalt not murder a child by abortion nor kill them when born." The latter part of the phrase probably refers to the widespread practice of infanticide in the Roman Empire: The mother would lay a newborn outside the home. If the father accepted responsibility for the child, he would pick it up and bring it into the house; otherwise, the child would be abandoned to die. The early Christian movement was known for its practice of scooping up such abandoned newborns and adopting them into their families. Roman pagans accused the Christians of collecting newborns in order to engage in rituals of human sacrifice.

Taking scripture as a whole the most we can say is that the Bible offers no clear statement against abortion and certainly nothing to support it. At the same time, this does not mean there is no moral basis for Christians' opposing abortion. On the contrary, the issue of when life begins is not settled by biblical texts. The advances of modern science have revealed many things about fetal development unknown in biblical times. Such research is an important factor in how Christians understand life, death, and the world around us. Although there may not be any consensus on the exact moment when life begins, as Robinson points out, modern science has shown that it is reasonable to believe it begins before the moment of birth.

At the same time, the lack of biblical imperatives does not mean that current abortion laws should be accepted without challenge by

Christians who disagree with them. We can believe that something is morally wrong without having any specific commandment forbidding it. Pacifist Christians, for example, have opposed war in spite of the fact that the Bible does not condemn it, Jesus' teaching about turning the other cheek notwithstanding. The fact that the Bible does not speak against abortion is not a basis for rejecting arguments against it, especially because we know that Christians from earlier centuries condemned it.

So where does this leave a Christian who is living with "clear ambiguity" on this issue? Let's attempt to find a place to stand for both sides of the issue (or perhaps two places).

An activist position for those who are against abortion in all circumstances is what can be called *prayerful resistance*. Prayerful resistance means putting into God's hands that which only God can accomplish, such as changing the minds and hearts of people, which is what is needed. Making abortion illegal treats the symptom, but not the problem. The reason for abortions is not laws that permit them or doctors who perform them. Both existed before *Roe* v. *Wade*. The root cause of abortions is human behavior, sometimes irresponsible, sometimes spawned by good intentions meshed with bad thinking, and sometimes carried out without forethought of the consequences that should have been weighed. Prayerful resistance offers Christians a way to witness to God's power to change people, but resists arguments that abortion on demand is a morally correct alternative. In other words, prayerful resistance is a position of trusting in the power of prayer to change circumstances that lead to the consideration of abortion. It asks, seeks, and knocks on the door of divine power to work its work in this life to lead people to make decisions that eliminate abortion as a viable choice for their lives. This does not mean that one does not demonstrate against abortion or is reluctant to speak against it. It only means that in the end Christians rely on God rather than civil law to stop abortions.

Let's turn now to the opposite end of the spectrum and talk about supporting the right of a woman to choose. First we should mention a few caveats regarding this position. One is that it is ethically responsible to support the right of choice while personally not believing in abortion on the basis of this issue's being one with multiple layers. Morality is only one dimension. In a democracy the issue of personal liberty is always hanging in the balance. Further, a nation that is intentionally secular cannot charge forth as if it can ignore this reality.

Second, many Christians find themselves with clear ambiguity on this issue. They are not ready to support absolute choice, but neither do they want abortions to be illegal across the board. Thus, the question is whether or not there is a position that bridges the extremes. I believe there is. It is called *choice with limits*. A primary reason that unqualified choice may be unacceptable is the fact that it opens the door to abortion's being used as a means of birth control, a position even the most liberal-minded Christian finds difficult to justify. As a young pastor, I faced parents who insisted their pregnant high school daughters have abortions, and in the process were unwittingly making a de facto statement that abortion was a legitimate means of birth control. Later, as a college chaplain, I encountered female students having multiple abortions, with the support of their boyfriends, who spoke openly about the abortions as if they were a reasonable answer to unwanted pregnancies.

Choice with limits offers support for a woman's right to choose but within reasonable boundaries—specifically, rape, incest, and the threat to a woman's life. Some might argue that anticipated birth defects fit within reasonable limits, but groups such as L'Arche communities for the severely mentally handicapped, in which persons with the most severe disabilities live with dignity and at the same time give and receive love in significant ways, make such decisions very problematic. Choice with limits attempts to strike a balance between life and rights. It takes seriously the physical and psychological impact both abortion and the lack of choice place on women. It is a position that promotes adoption when the above criteria are not present, but it also walks the line between living in a religiously neutral nation and holding religious convictions that contradict current law. Perhaps most important, choice with limits serves as a witness to Christians' being a people who can balance the integrity of their convictions with the realities of a religiously neutral democratic society. Choice with limits will not satisfy those on either extreme, but it is an extended hand toward those open-minded Christians who oppose abortion.

In spite of the distance separating prayerful resistance and choice with limits, these positions are both close enough to the center to create the possibility of sharing common ground on a few points of mutual interest. The first is the importance of consistency. Emerson may have been correct when he said, "A foolish consistency is the hobgoblin of little minds, adored by little statesmen and philosophers and divines,"[23] but what we are talking about is no small consistency. It's not that inconsistency renders a position invalid. It's that recognizing it invites reexamination. Whenever opposing views continue to refine their respective points of view, the opportunity for dialogue increases. On the issue of abortion, inconsistencies on both sides reaffirm the reality that no one has a corner on truth in this matter. Pro-life advocates are often the strongest supporters of capital punishment, saying that a woman has no right to end a pregnancy but the state has every right to end the life of a fully grown person. The Catholic Church is the primary exception to this inconsistency among anti-abortionists. It makes a direct correlation between its opposition to abortion and its opposition to capital punishment: "Abolition of capital punishment is also a manifestation of our belief in the unique worth and dignity of each person from the moment of conception, a creature made in the image and likeness of God."[24]

On the other side, many pro-choice advocates are at the same time the strongest voices against capital punishment. On the face of it there would appear to be no inconsistency, because pro-choice supporters do not believe that life begins until birth. Yet many support choice and also acknowledge that life may in fact begin before birth. Some even support choice on the basis of personal freedom rather than on support for abortion itself. But in either case a stand against capital punishment puts them in an unavoidable conflict. Their support of choice is a position that places rights above morality. But their opposition to capital punishment does just the opposite. It places morality above society's right to avenge itself. Herein lies the inconsistency that weakens their position on both issues, which is similar to the position in which pro-life people find themselves. Both sides might move closer to the center of the debate if they would take these inconsistencies (and there are others, as we shall see) into account when promoting their respective agendas. At least doing so might make attitudes a bit less strident and a bit more civil.

This leads to a second possible point of common ground, which is a commitment to civility for the sake of reconciliation. This is a special need among those who advocate prayerful resistance. Inflammatory speech fans the flames of the extremism that encourages people such as Paul Hill, who was convicted of the first-degree murders of workers at an abortion clinic in Pensacola, Florida, to take action. Calling women who agonize over abortion decisions murderers places them in the same category as the Florida escaped convicts who shot a policeman in cold blood. It doesn't seem much of a stretch to understand that this kind of language not only represents careless thinking but also reveals a callous heart far removed from the heart of Jesus. Pro-choice advocates need to watch their words as well, but at this point inflammatory speech is more of a problem within anti-abortion groups. It seems that all Christians could agree that such speech pushes people apart, hindering the potential for reconciliation.

A third point is the recognition that men are not extraneous to abortion decisions. Married men or the male partner in an unmarried couple for whom sex was consensual are directly involved and should be given a place at the table where decisions for or against abortion are made. The consequences and responsibilities for conceptions arising from consensual sex should be borne by both partners. This is certainly the view our society takes toward deadbeat dads. It seems at least disingenuous to argue that deadbeat dads should be brought to justice while denying men a role in abortion decisions. A more reasonable position is that consensual sex is itself de facto agreement for both people to share equal responsibility in such a decision. Practically, this means the desire by either partner not to abort should be respected, except when a woman's life is at risk.

Fourth, it would seem that all Christians could agree that there is no moral basis for late-term abortions, again excepting times when the mother's life is at stake. Calling for early decisions for abortion within the limits we have suggested places no unjust burden on a woman to make a decision. Nor is it an infringement on a woman's freedom to eliminate abortion as an option when fetal survivability outside the womb becomes possible. Except in the case of the risk to a woman's life, one is hard-pressed as a person of faith to make the case for late-term abortions.

These four points seem to me to offer a reasonable place for opposing sides on abortion to meet as they live out the commitment to the ministry of reconciliation. These points do not impinge on the freedom to engage in prayerful resistance to abortion and allow for limited choice under special circumstances. Both positions reflect different ways to live as a Christian within a secular world. As such, each offers a place to stand that balances commitment to communal standards and individual rights within particular circumstances.

There is more to capital punishment than meets the eye.

By the late 1960s the death penalty had been virtually abandoned by all states while they waited for further rulings from the U.S. Supreme Court, which, had it followed the established trend, could have eliminated capital punishment altogether. But in 1976 the nation's highest court reinstated it in the case of *Gregg* v. *the state of Georgia,* ruling that the death penalty does not invariably violate the U. S. Constitution if administered in a manner designed to guard against arbitrariness and discrimination. Since that time thirty-eight states have reinstated capital punishment, the exceptions being Alaska, the District of Columbia, Hawaii, Iowa, Maine, Massachusetts, Michigan, Minnesota, North Dakota, Rhode Island, Vermont, West Virginia, and Wisconsin. In thirteen states, the minimum age for imposing capital punishment is eighteen; in four it is age seventeen; in nine it is age sixteen; and in twelve states no minimum age has been established. In 1996 Mississippi prosecutors sought the death penalty for a thirteen-year-old boy. In Indiana ten-year-olds can be tried as adults and, if convicted, can be sentenced to death.

Further, in 1999, 98 persons in twenty states were executed: 35 in Texas; 14 in Virginia; 9 in Missouri; 7 in Arizona; 6 in Oklahoma; 4 each in Arkansas, North Carolina, and South Carolina; 2 each in Alabama, California, and Delaware; and 1 each in Florida, Illinois, Indiana, Kentucky, Louisiana, Nevada, Ohio, Pennsylvania, and Utah. Of the persons executed in 1999, 61 were Caucasian, 33 were African American, 2 were Native American, and 2 were Asian American; all of those executed in 1999 were men; 94 of the executions in 1999 were carried out by lethal injection, 3 by electrocution, and 1 by lethal gas.

The racial makeup of current death row inmates is as follows: African Americans make up half of the death row populations in Virginia, North Carolina, South Carolina, Mississippi, Ohio, and Delaware, and more than two-thirds in Pennsylvania, Illinois, and Louisiana. In addition, three out of four people waiting to be executed in federal and U.S. military prisons are African American. In California and Texas more than 60 percent of the people currently on death row are either African American, Latino, Asian American, or Native American.[25]

While the court has said that the death penalty must be administered in a fair way to be legal, meeting that criterion does not necessarily mean it is moral, and for Christians morality is the key issue. But unlike our earlier discussions, wherein the Bible's virtual silence proved to be a sticking point, one might wish this were the case when it comes to capital punishment. Indeed, much of what the Bible says about it is deeply troubling. Torah law is very explicit about offenses punishable by death, including such offenses as murder, kidnapping, a child cursing his or her parents, blasphemy, flagrant violations of the Sabbath, and all manner of sexual offenses (see Leviticus 20). These offenses fall into two classes: (1) crimes against persons and (2) crimes of sacrilege. The methods for putting someone to death were extremely brutal. Stoning involved throwing the person off a high platform. If the fall did not kill the person, then he or she was stoned. Burning was a process of "putting someone to the fire" in a particularly horrible way. The person was tied to a stake, the mouth forced open, and molten lead poured down the throat.

These commandments in Torah were so troubling that Talmudic rabbis of later generations resisted following them based on their commitment to the sanctity of life. Sometimes their opposition led them to interpret the Torah commandments to mean death by divine intervention rather than death imposed by a court.

They also "devised a system of technicalities to prevent the conviction of a defendant for a capital crime."[26] Frankly, the notion that capital punishment is justified today because of Torah law is an absurdity beyond measure. No one with wits intact would advocate killing people for the reasons found in Torah or using the methods by which the deed was carried out back then.

The New Testament does not mention the death penalty. Jesus makes no direct reference to it. He rejects the Torah's ethic of an "eye for an eye" for individuals and, further, says that his followers are to turn the other cheek and love rather than hate their enemies (Mt. 5:38–44). But whether or not this constitutes a rejection of the Torah's teaching on capital punishment is unclear. His charge to the Pharisees wanting to stone the woman caught in adultery that only those without sin should do so (Jn. 8:7) showed displeasure over self-righteousness, but if this constitutes a statement that rejects the Torah's law on the death penalty, it is a very indirect one.

Yet we may not be without any guidance at all on the subject. From our perspective today we can interpret the trial and death of Jesus as a telling example of the potential injustice of capital punishment's putting innocent persons to death. So, too, with the stoning of the Christian witness Stephen (Acts 7:54–60), whose only crime was to talk about Jesus.

This kind of injustice continues today. In 1987 Albert Ronnie Burrell was tried, convicted, and sentenced to death for killing an elderly couple in rural Louisiana. At one point he was seventeen days from execution. On January 2, 2001, he was released from prison because two persistent attorneys who came across his case finally proved that he had been falsely convicted, because "people that we all trust—police, prosecutors, the system—failed."[27]

His case is not an isolated one. In the past twenty years, 350 capital offense convictions were later determined to be mistakes, but the determinations came too late for twenty-five innocent people who had already been executed.[28] To argue that injustices of this nature are the price society must pay to protect its own is woefully lacking in moral power to persuade. Indeed, in 2000, conservative Governor George Ryan (R-Illinois) halted executions in his state after it was determined that a man who was almost put to death was innocent. Said Ryan, "People are starting to understand there's a possibility innocent people are going to be put to death. I don't think anybody wants that on their hands or their consciences."[29]

The reason for this trend toward halting executions is the terrible state of the justice system in this country. Prosecutors suppress evidence that points to the innocence of someone they are prosecuting because it would be embarrassing for the prosecution or the police. Court-appointed attorneys often do very little to research their clients' cases. As in Ronnie Burrell's case, the system is broken, and innocent people sometimes pay with their lives. From 1973 to 1995, 68 percent of death penalty convictions were reversed because of problems in the capital punishment system in the states involved.

These factors suggest that the question of justice is a primary concern with capital punishment. The death of innocent people, especially when coupled with the ability of some guilty people to pay for the best legal counsel and thus gain their freedom (O.J. Simpson comes to mind), underscores the need for those Christians who support the death penalty to answer more than a few morals questions that cannot be dismissed. In the end the question remains as stated in a 1984 Tennessee Conference of Catholic Bishops statement: "Is it right to kill people who kill people in order to show that killing people is wrong?"

But what about deterrence? Would that justify its use? Perhaps, if there were reliable evidence that it is in fact a deterrent, but the evidence suggests otherwise. States that have the death penalty have higher civilian murder rates than those that do not. The average murder rate per 100,000 people in states with capital punishment is about 8 percent, while it is only 4.4 percent in states without capital punishment.[30]

The question, then, is whether or not there are any moral grounds on which to stand in support of capital punishment. The honest answer is no, not without serious problems, but one possibility is that capital punishment is a right of a religiously neutral society, as long as the following stipulations are satisfied: (1) that no one under twenty-one years of age can be sentenced to death; (2) that the crime meets the test of law; (3) that the police investigation and trial be above reproach in regard to equal protection under the law; (4) that the standard of guilt be raised from "beyond a reasonable doubt" to "beyond a shadow of doubt";

and (5) that the right of appeal be fully utilized within a reasonable timetable.

The reality, of course, is that the likelihood of all the above criteria being met is remote. For this reason it would seem that *the moral high ground for Christians is to oppose capital punishment in support of life in prison without parole as the most just punishment a society can deliver to its citizens.* As the Catholic Bishops argue, "Abolition of the death penalty would promote values that are important to us as citizens and as Christians."[31] Moreover, Jesus told the Pharisees ready to stone the adulterous woman to let the one among them who was without sin cast the first stone (Jn. 8:7). It would go beyond his intentions to say that Jesus was against people paying for their crimes. But it does seem reasonable to believe he was saying that justice should always be tempered with an awareness of the sinful nature of all human beings, including those who have the responsibility of enforcing the law in just ways. Life without parole might err on the side of caution in remembering his words, but it is at least a way to guard against innocent people being put to death.

Church and state need protection from each other.

An attempt has been made in the discussions thus far to serve the goal of open-mindedness by walking a fine line between opposing views. But the issue of prayer in public schools presents us with a different challenge. Here the question is whether or not Christians can support the U.S. Constitution. Supreme Court rulings in this area have been amazingly consistent, albeit their implications at times have been vague, in rejecting any form of school-sponsored prayer. Article 6, paragraph 3, of the U.S. Constitution states:

> The senators and representatives before-mentioned, and the members of the several state legislatures, and all executive and judicial officers, both of the United States and of the several states, shall be bound by oath or affirmation, to support this constitution; but no religious test shall ever be required as a qualification to any office or public trust under the United States.

The First Amendment, usually called the Establishment Clause goes further in declaring:

> Congress shall make no law respecting an establishment of religion, or prohibiting the free exercise thereof; or abridging the freedom of speech, or of the press; or the right of the people peaceably to assemble, and to petition the Government for a redress of grievances.

For years both liberal and conservatives courts have ruled against the once-common practice of classroom prayer in public schools on the basis of the Establishment Clause. It might be helpful to review what some of the most important rulings have actually said.[32]

— ILLINOIS V. MCCOLLUM (1948)
(Teacher Providing Religious Instruction)

The court ruled that religious teachers providing religious instruction in public schools violated the Establishment Clause of the First Amendment of the U.S. Constitution.

— ZORACH V. CLAUSON (1952)
(Off-campus Religious Training)

The court said that it is constitutional for students to leave campus to receive religious training, making special consideration and allowances for religious training constitutional.

— ENGEL V. VITALE (1962)
(Government-written Prayers)

During the tenure of Chief Justice Earl Warren the Supreme Court decided that nondenominational prayers written by government officials violated the Establishment Clause. Government officials represent the government, and the government cannot establish religion.

— SCHOOL DISTRICT V. SCHEMPP (1963)
(The Lord's Prayer in Public Schools)

The Warren Court, making the first Supreme Court decision specifically related to prayer in school, also ruled against the reciting of the "Lord's Prayer" in public schools, arguing that although it did not force a government prayer on students, it did qualify as a government agency's promoting religion and, thus, violated the Establishment Clause.

— STONE V. GRAHAM (1980)
(The Ten Commandments in Public School Classrooms)

A Kentucky law requiring the posting of the Ten Commandments in all public school classrooms was ruled unconstitutional. The court also developed guidelines that required that a law must have a secular purpose, neither promoting nor suppressing religion, and it must not mingle government and religion.

— MARSH V. CHAMBERS (1983)
(Prayers in Legislative Sessions)

The court determined that it is constitutional for legislatures to open sessions with prayer, because it's traditional and doesn't constitute the establishment of religion.

— LYNCH V. DONNELLY (1984)
(City-sponsored Religious Displays)

The court ruled that a city display of a nativity scene did not violate the Constitution as long as nonreligious Christmas symbols, such as reindeer and images of Santa Claus, were included.

— WALLACE V. JEFFERY (1985)
(Public School Prayer)

Because the Alabama legislature refused to argue their points on nonreligious terms, the court determined that the Alabama law allowing teachers to set aside time for meditation and voluntary prayer was motivated by the will to promote religion and was therefore unconstitutional.

— BOARD OF EDUCATION V. MERGENS (1990)
(Extracurricular Religious Groups at Public Schools)

The court upheld a federal law that gave student groups, including religious groups, equal access to high school premises.

— LEE V. WEISMAN (1992)
(Public School Prayer)

The court said that school-sponsored prayers at official school functions violate the Establishment Clause. It was determined that the Constitution guarantees that the government cannot coerce anyone to support or participate in religion or its exercise.

— SANTA FE INDEPENDENT SCHOOL DISTRICT V. DOE (2000)

On June 19, 2000, the U.S. Supreme Court decision said that school athletic events are school-sponsored activities, and that public prayers of any kind during them violated the Establishment Clause. The court made clear that there is not one Constitution for football players and one for all other public-school students.

None of these rulings has settled all the questions that swirl around programs and policies in public schools across the land. Many of them have clearly answered one question without providing clarity on tangential ones. The best guideline school officials have is what is called "the lemon test." It consists of three things: (1) The program, policy, or event must have a secular or educational purpose; (2) it can neither advance nor inhibit religion; and (3) it cannot entangle the state in religion. Decisions based on these three factors are obviously discretionary to some extent. School attorneys themselves confess to using "the cringe" rule of thumb. If something creates a constitutional "cringe" in them, it probably shouldn't be done. Yet within these somewhat amorphous guidelines the courts have given straightforward answers to the question regarding prayer in public schools. That answer has been an unequivocal no to anything that even hints at official school sponsorship, endorsement, or permission that forces a student to opt out of it, the Santa Fe ruling noted above being a case in point.

There are a few important points to remember about these court rulings. One is that no individual or group is prevented from praying on its own. So the short answer to the question, Can students pray in school? is yes. The only restriction is that it be done in a way that does not force it on others. Second, no religious individual or group is prevented from influencing political discussion and decision making. Since the courts' rulings against prayer in public schools, political involvement of religious groups of all stripes has increased dramatically; perhaps the two developments are not unrelated. Third, the courts have stated without equivocation that federal and state governments are bound by the Constitution to be religiously neutral. The net effect is that we have a government that protects the right of every person to hold and practice or not to hold or practice religious convictions. The Constitution does not allow the government to develop any affiliation with or show any favoritism toward one religion over another or toward any religion at all. This means that even though the U.S. has a majority of Christians, that fact does not change the constitutional neutrality of the state.

The position of some Christian groups and politicians in response to these court rulings has been to seek to overturn them legislatively. They believe they violate the "free exercise" part of the Establishment Clause. One of Newt Gingrich's first moves as Speaker of the House before his fall from grace and power was to propose a "religious freedom" amendment:

> Nothing in this Constitution shall be construed to prohibit individual or group prayer in public schools or other public institutions. No person shall be required by the United States or by any State to participate in prayer. Neither the United States nor any State shall compose the words of any prayer to be said in public schools.[33]

An amendment requires a two-thirds majority in both the House and the Senate and a three-fourths majority of all state legislatures. Gingrich's proposal failed to make it out of the House.

Not to be deterred, Rep. Ernest Istook (R-Oklahoma) and Sen. James Inhofe (R-Oklahoma) proposed similar measures:

> To secure the people's right to acknowledge God: The right
> to pray or acknowledge religious belief, heritage or
> tradition on public property, including public schools, shall
> not be infringed. The government shall not compel joining
> in prayer, initiate or compose school prayers, discriminate
> against or deny a benefit on account of religion.[34]

This measure also failed. But our question here is whether or not
such efforts define faithfulness to the gospel and/or reflect a
commitment to being open-minded Christians. If we turn to
scripture for help, we find that Jesus didn't address the issue of
prayer in schools directly, of course, but he did speak to the issue of
the relationship of Christians to a secular government. To Pharisees
who asked him if they should pay taxes to the emperor, Jesus said:
"Give therefore to the emperor the things that are the emperor's,
and to God the things that are God's" (Mt. 22:21). Although all
things belong to God, on Earth some things also belong to the
emperor. Jesus told his listeners to make sure they know which is
which, and then give to each what each is due. The guide for doing
so is that ultimate things belong to God (first commandment). That
is, Christians owe their ultimate loyalty to God first. "Strive first for
the kingdom of God" is the way Jesus said it (Mt. 6:33). Essentially,
Jesus was saying what scripture as a whole declares: The state is not
God, and God is not the state.

It would seem that the founders of this nation understood this.
Both Thomas Jefferson and James Madison believed that a strict
separation between church and state was mandatory if the new
nation was to avoid the pitfalls of the state/church collaboration
common in Europe. Together they were successful in the drafting
and passage of the Virginia Statute of Religious Freedom that
became the basis for the First Amendment to the U.S. Constitution.
The phrase "wall of separation" comes from Jefferson, who used it
as a summary statement of the Establishment Clause when, as
President, he responded to a letter from the Westbury Baptists in
Danbury, Connecticut, who were being persecuted by
Congregationalists:

> Believing with you that religion is a matter which lies solely
> between man and his God; that he owes account to none

other for this faith or his worship; that the legislative powers of the government reach actions only, not opinions, I contemplate with sovereign reverence that act of the whole American people which declared that their legislature should "make no law respecting an establishment of religions, or prohibiting the free exercise thereof," thus building *a wall of separation* [emphasis added] between church and state.[35]

What is most interesting in regard to prayer in public schools is the fact that Jefferson and Madison worked together to ensure this "wall of separation" for quite different reasons. Jefferson feared religious intolerance. In his first inaugural address he said,

> Though the will of the majority is in all cases to prevail... that will to be rightful must be reasonable; that the minority possesses their equal rights, which equal law must protect, and to violate would be oppression...Let us, then, fellow citizens, unite with one heart and one mind. Let us restore to social intercourse that harmony and affection without which liberty and life itself are but dreary things.[36]

Jefferson believed that the key to harmonious social discourse was the recognition that a difference in opinions did not constitute a difference in principles by which a people governed themselves. The need to expunge political intolerance from the young nation's temperament, he said, was all the more important for not "having banished from our land that religious intolerance under which mankind so long bled and suffered."[37]

Madison, on the other hand, being a committed Christian, feared state infringement on the free exercise of religion. The state that gives is the state that can take away. Madison supported a state and federal guarantee that government would have no such discretionary power. Based on this history, it is a reasonable conjecture that both Madison and Jefferson would cringe today at any of the numerous entanglements that currently exist between church and state. Certainly they would view a prayer in public schools as not only violating but undermining the Establishment Clause they helped to formulate and enact. In their assessment a wall of separation serves the interests of both church and state by protecting the one from the other.

Another reason to believe that it serves the church not to promote prayer in schools is the fact that religiously neutral prayers that could meet constitutional requirements would be innocuous, if not offensive, to the convictions we hold. As someone has said, such a prayer would be something like, "May God, Buddha, Krishna, Cosmic Consciousness, and all that is, bless you." What purpose would a prayer of this nature serve? It would not even address the concern that there is antireligious sentiment in the public realm. Certainly those truly interested in the winsomeness and witness of their own faith traditions would not consider this kind of generic prayer worthy of the struggle to have it.

Along with this factor is the history of prayer in public schools. The older part of the Baby Boom generation grew up with prayer in schools. It was a common daily activity for children to recite the Pledge of Allegiance and the Lord's Prayer. On occasion a Bible passage was read aloud by the teacher. This is the same generation that gave birth to both the benefits and excesses of the sexual revolution and that challenged all institutional authority. This history makes one wonder why advocates of prayer in public schools believe it would help in any way to restore the kind of moral order in American life in which they believe.

A fifth reason you can believe current court rulings are appropriate is that the gospel itself invites Christians to model genuine sensitivity to the fear people of other faiths have regarding Christian efforts to get prayer into public schools. In a recent newspaper article, attorney and Harvard professor Alan Dershowitz wrote,

> The very first act of the new Bush administration was to have a Protestant Evangelist minister officially dedicate the inauguration to Jesus Christ, whom he declared to be "our savior." Invoking the Father, the Son, the Lord Jesus Christ, and "the Holy Spirit," Billy Graham's son, the man selected by George W. Bush to bless his presidency, excluded tens of millions of Jews, Buddhists, Shintoists, Unitarians, agnostics and atheists from his blessing by his particularistic and parochial language...

The inauguration ended with another Protestant minister inviting all who agree that Jesus is "the Christ" to say, "Amen"...Sen. Joseph Lieberman, D-Conn., along with many others who do not believe that Jesus is the messiah, was put in the position of either denying his own faith or remaining silent while others around him said, "Amen." This is precisely the position in which public-school students are placed when "voluntary" prayer is conducted at school events. If they join in prayer inconsistent with their religious beliefs, they have been coerced into violating their conscience. If they leave or refuse to join, they stand out as different. No student should be put in that position by their public schools, just as no public official should be placed in that situation by their government at an inauguration.[38]

The Central Conference of American Rabbis has expressed similar sentiments: "The CCAR confirms its long-standing commitment to the principle of the separation of church and state, as historically understood by the First Amendment to the Constitution...and deplores these attempts to compromise a basic principle that has served for over two centuries as the cornerstone of religious liberty."[39]

When we think about Christian persecution of Jews and other non-Christians throughout history, which helped to make Hitler's "final solution to the Jewish problem" possible, it is not difficult to understand such fears about efforts to abridge or abrogate the First Amendment. It would be a positive sign that we have learned the lessons of history if Christians today demonstrated sensitivity to these fears.

The final reason to believe that a wall of separation should exist between church and state, including in the issue of school prayer, is the very important responsibility Christians—and all religious communities—have for teaching the faith to their children. Christians should be able to affirm the view of the Union of American Hebrew Congregations, a Reform Jewish organization, when it says it "cherishes the conviction that the maintenance and furtherance of religion are the responsibility of the synagogue, the church and the home, and not any agency of the government, including the public schools."[40] There is no advantage—and no small danger—in having public officials who are not trained to do so train, teach, or promote Christianity or any other faith tradition.

What seems clear, then, is that the current case law regarding prayer in public schools is something for which Christians can be enthusiastically supportive. Madison and Jefferson were correct. State and church need protection from each other. School-sponsored prayer could open the door to the state's intrusion into other religious matters. At the same time it could make the state vulnerable to undue influence from the church in state matters and could evolve into religious intolerance. The way to ensure state-free religion is not to accept state favors. Prayer in public schools would be such a favor. When Jesus distinguished between what is God's and what belongs to the emperor, he was at least suggesting that the state may not be a friend of faith. In his day it wasn't. It would be naive to think it is today, except as it serves the needs of the state, not the church. Protecting the state from the church also protects the church from the state.

6

What You Can Believe about Other Religions

The issue of church and state opens the door to the question of Christianity's relationship to other religions. While current surveys report that the majority of Americans identify themselves as Christian, the United States has increasingly become a religiously plural society.[1] This is because a religiously neutral government such as ours not only allows for but also de facto creates an environment of competing religious claims. However, it has not been until recently that Christianity has encountered the reality that it is not the only kid on the block, so to speak, in terms of influence and power. Once upon a time Christians went unchallenged in determining local community policies and practices, from prayer in public schools to sermons preached at high school assemblies to holidays being scheduled around the church year. That has now changed. As never before, a nonreligious and non-Christian religious presence has emerged to make successful court challenges across the land and bring a halt to Christian dominance (see previous chapter). Despite the debate that continues over these actions, one thing is now clear. Christianity is not the only religious alternative for people hungering for spiritual fulfillment and growth.

This new day for Christians in this country confronts us with an issue of our attitude toward other religions. What are we to think about them, and how are we to act toward them? What kind of relationship can we have with them? Is it possible to have a positive one without giving up basic beliefs that define who we are as Christians? The primary answers to these questions up to now have reflected two quite opposite attitudes. One is that Christianity is the only true faith and that all others are either false or to be fulfilled in Christianity. The great commission (Mt. 28:18–20) is understood to be marching orders for Christians to seek and to save the lost, including people of other faiths. From this perspective the validity of other religious traditions is rejected out of hand, end of discussion. The church is the repository of the only true faith by which people can be saved from ultimate condemnation.

At the opposite end of the spectrum is the view that Christianity is only one among many ways God works in the world. Therefore, the validity of other religious traditions is both implicitly and explicitly accepted by these more liberal thinking Christians. Inclusiveness is valued over exclusive Christian claims.

Both views have major weaknesses.

Lukewarm faith is not limited to an ancient city in Asia Minor.

In John's Revelation a stern warning is given to the church in Laodicea about lukewarm discipleship (3:14–22). Being lukewarm is worse than being hot or cold, mainly because it makes both commitment and opposition to it not worth the effort.

Ironically, the virtue of tolerance, especially in regard to religious pluralism, can fall prey to this problem when strong convictions are seen as contradictory to it. Once a student of mine said that he could not extend an invitation to discipleship at the close of a worship service because it could be offensive to members of other faiths who might be present. This is an example of a failure to understand the difference between tolerance and lukewarmness. Lukewarmness may stem from a simple lack of conviction, but it may also fill the vacuum created when one believes that an attitude of inclusiveness means hiding the light of one's faith. Rather than showing respect for others, this kind of inclusiveness actually shows just the opposite. It assumes that those of other traditions cannot accept differences or understand strength in convictions. This is the danger of open-mindedness that is not grounded in strong faith, and it leads to timidity replacing witnessing and evangelism being abandoned in the name of tolerance.

But, of course, the opposite is also a danger. It is the view that exclusivity is an inevitable dimension of faithful discipleship. The history of Christian intolerance is a more than sufficient reminder of the consequences of this kind of thinking. But the problem is not simply one that existed in the past. Intolerance remains entrenched and ready to raise its ugly head whenever a threat to Christian dominance is perceived. Those most passionate about public school prayer or posting the Ten Commandments in courthouses are almost exclusively Christian, yet they would certainly not support a daily school reading from the Islamic Koran or the Hindu Bhagavad Gita. In the 2001 session of the Minnesota state legislature, Representative Arlon Lindner, previously criticized by colleagues for anti-Semitic comments, sent an e-mail to them stating his opposition to the Dalai Lama of Tibet speaking to a joint session of the house and senate during his visit to the Twin Cities. His letter stated that he viewed Buddhism as a cult "incompatible with Christian principles."[2]

None of these past or current actions in themselves makes Christian truth claims invalid, but they do reflect a consistent pattern of intolerance, one consequence of which has been to undercut the credibility of the Christian witness in the world. This is not something to be taken lightly. A Christian faith that refuses to understand the need for credibility is one that will grow increasingly inward and selfish and will be marginalized more often by the larger culture. Perhaps the first step on the road to a healthier attitude toward people of other faiths is the need for Christians to acknowledge the sins we have committed in the name of Jesus. Such admission would be a clear sign that divine grace has finally humbled us. Moreover, it would signal that we accept the reality that salvation is a gift God gives because of who God is rather than who we are. Herein are the seeds of greater tolerance and understanding of other religions. The need for strong faith and an open mind are never more needed than when it comes to the attitude Christians have toward people of other religions. What it would mean to embody this kind of faith and attitude is precisely the question we shall now seek to answer.

A little knowledge can go a long way.

Informed Christian commitment begins at the point of a thorough knowledge of our faith in Jesus Christ as both man and Savior. He is the content of the Christian faith. Neither lukewarmness nor intolerance can thrive where there is knowledge or understanding of him, what he actually said, and how he challenged the legalism of Judaism, spoke against religious hypocrisy and a loveless kind of piety, and openly defied Jewish exclusivism that gave people the right to define God in absolute terms. Jesus said that he did not come to judge others who do not follow his teachings, but that the teachings themselves would serve as judge (Jn. 12:47–48). From the beginning Christians have failed to realize that his words apply as much to them as anyone else. The more we know what Jesus said and did, the less likely we will be to condemn those who are of other faith traditions. Further, we will become more ready to challenge religious intolerance in any form toward anyone.

Fear is no match for divine love.

The closer we get to Jesus, the less fear we will have about people of other faiths. This is why the early Christians could face their fears. Were they right about Jesus, or were they wrong? What about their brothers and sisters who chose not to follow him? Why hadn't things worked out the way they had envisioned? Questions reflect fears and at the same time exacerbate them. And fears lie at the root of exclusivism. Many Christians fear the validity of other faith traditions because such validity would challenge the core of what they have been taught to believe. Their faith is one that depends on the invalidity of other religions. Lines are drawn in the sand; rules become more important than people; and hypocrisy abounds, not because these people fail to live by the rules they set, but because they fail to admit that the rules expose their own weaknesses. This failure entrenches their fears, and the cycle is repeated again and again.

This is the environment in which I grew up. I was taught that the Bible says Jesus is the only way to salvation (Jn. 14:6; Acts 4:12). Thus, all non-Christians were doomed to hell unless they became Christian. What my Sunday school teachers did not realize is that they had turned faith into "works salvation" and then failed the test themselves because of their own sins. They did not understand that grace is based on God's actions, not human response, that the salvation through grace God revealed in Jesus could be as large and encompassing as God chose it to be, and that John's gospel says that it includes the entire world (3:16–17). Instead of faith in Jesus being the doorway to new life for me as a young Christian, I was told that faith in Jesus makes salvation the exclusive claim of Christians. That meant, of course, that a classmate who was the son of the local rabbi was going to hell. So was a Hindu man named Gandhi, who I had learned in school had freed India from British colonialism through passive resistance.

None of this made any sense at the time, but it did fill me with the fear that should any of these people get into heaven, it would mean Jesus was not the Son of God. It was not unlike the fear of integration instilled in me by these same people, who were convinced it would lead to intermarriage, among other things that were "obviously" bad. It was not until young adulthood that I understood from scripture how contradictory these fears were to what Jesus was all about. Even then, intellectual freedom outdistanced emotional freedom. It was only when I learned that the eradication of all fear is not a human act, but is ultimately and finally an act of divine love, that I was finally free from it.

> God is love, and those who abide in love abide in God, and God abides in them. Love has been perfected among us in this: that we may have boldness on the day of judgment, because as he is, so are we in this world. There is no fear in love, but perfect love casts out fear; for fear has to do with punishment, and whoever fears has not reached perfection in love. We love because he first loved us. (1 Jn. 4:16b–19)

This truth brought relief to a fearful heart, because I was able to trust the judging of others to the same love and mercy with which I would be judged. Divine love always brings us to our knees in humbleness, and through our own weakness reveals the reality of inescapable human limitations. It is precisely then that we reach a deeper level of trust in God. Tolerance is no longer seen as betrayal, but as a quality of Christian discipleship. Nor is it confused with a timidity of heart that undercuts commitment in the name of being inclusive. But most important, divine love frees Christians to delight in the joy of faith. Joy is inversely proportional to fear. The less fear there is, the more joy there is. Being Christian is supposed to lead to joy (Jn. 15:11). Fear is its enemy. Love is the antidote to fear. There is no joy in condemning others. There is joy in witnessing to the love that has changed and is changing our lives. And the more joy we have, the more open we are to learning about other faiths and the people who witness to the best about them. When we do not fear and we have much joy, we are open to new learning that expands our horizons and deepens commitment to our own faith.

One such new learning for open-minded Christians is to understand that if salvation is the gift of God, then it is reasonable to think that a person can believe in the God whose salvation work was embodied in Jesus without believing in Jesus, and in that faith in the God of Jesus receive the gift of salvation. As we have already said, what God has done in Jesus, God has done. Believing this to be true or not does not alter the reality of it. The work of God and human faith are related, but not one and the same. Christians rightly proclaim Jesus as Savior. But as Savior he points to God who made him Savior through the resurrection. Should there be people who trust themselves to God without understanding or believing in what God has done in Jesus, I suspect Jesus will be the first to welcome them into the kingdom. As for people who do not believe, it is enough to leave them in the hands of a loving and gracious God.

Open-minded also means open-hearted.

Jesus once said, "I have other sheep that do not belong to this fold" (Jn. 10:16). The text probably refers to Gentiles, but it speaks directly to the relationship of Christians to other religions. God's heart is bigger than most of us understand. The temptation to draw circles that limit rather than include is always present. But Jesus was one who included others often thought to be the ones who should be left out. For open-minded Christians the lesson in his actions is to leave the circles to God and focus on loving Jesus. That is the best way to learn how to love the way he loved. To be radically committed to loving him will expand rather than limit our vision of love. In my own tradition there is an ecumenical statement that declares, "We are Christians only, but not the only Christians." The presence of other religions and the love of God revealed in Jesus Christ together invite an expansion of this statement to say, "We are the people of God only, but not the only people of God."

But what about the great commission? What about evangelism? It is a matter of how we understand both. Evangelism is not converting others to Jesus Christ. It is witnessing to our own commitment to him. The Spirit changes people's hearts; we don't. The great commission is a call to teach others about Jesus. We do that in several ways, one of which is through an attitude of tolerance and understanding toward other faiths. Rather than a compromise, this is a powerful witness to the kind of person discipleship has made of us. Thus, we can be as Christian as we can be while trusting the effect of that witness to the Holy Spirit.

We began this book with a call to open-mindedness, but in the end we see that even that is too limited. The call is to become bold Christians who are not only open-minded but also open-hearted.

Notes

—— Introduction ——

[1]Clarence Darrow and William Jennings Bryan, 20 July 1925, *State of Tennessee v. John Scopes*, as quoted in "Arguments for the Ages: Darrow and Bryan at the Scopes Trial," *Minneapolis Star Tribune*, 6 November 2000, editorial page.

[2]*Minneapolis Star Tribune*, 13 June 2000, sec. A, 5.

[3]Marcus Borg's *Meeting Jesus Again for the First Time* (San Francisco: HarperSanFrancisco-HarperCollins Paperback Edition, 1995) has been received positively in many mainline churches. The work of John Dominick Crossan has been praised for its fresh and careful study of Jesus by some scholars who reject his conclusions; see N. T. Wright's critique of Crossan and more positive assessment of Borg in *Jesus and the Victory of God* (Minneapolis: Fortress Press, 1996), 44–78.

[4]While the Jesus Seminar members speak for themselves, as a group they seemed to have concluded that the gospel of Mark is a work of fiction, that the gospel of Thomas and the material called Q are collections of Jesus' sayings only (a disputable point) from an earlier time than the New Testament canon and therefore more reliable, and that the New Testament gospels are a "Christian overlay" of the original gospel that "probably consisted only of a collection of pronouncements attributed to Jesus, in which his birth, death, and resurrection played no role at all" (Robert W. Funk, *Honest to Jesus* [San Francisco: HarperSanFrancisco, 1996], 135.) See also N. T. Wright, *The New Testament and the People of God* (Minneapolis: Fortress Press, 1992) for an insightful study of the nature of knowledge and the historical context of first-century Judaism and the early church. Wright believes that the New Testament gospels can stand up under the best of historical scrutiny because it is a false dichotomy to separate faith from history, fact from values, religion from politics, and nature from supernature. He believes that the more Christians understand the first-century Judaism into which Jesus was born, by which he was nurtured, and with which he ultimately clashed, the better we will understand the Jesus we believe was and is the Son of God. His thoughtful scholarship reflects the best definition of theology, which is "faith seeking understanding." He also believes that the search for the historical Jesus will make the church healthier, observing: "If church leaders themselves spent more time studying and teaching Jesus and the Gospels, a good many of the other things we worry about in day-to-day church life would be seen in their proper light...I believe...that each generation has to wrestle with the question of Jesus...that we should discover more and more who Jesus was and is, precisely in order to be equipped to engage with the world he came to serve" (31). He then adds, "All our historical study...must be done to energize the church and its mission in the world" (Ibid.). Thus, contrary to the views of many of his colleagues, he believes that the biblical writers just might have accurately understood who Jesus truly was. A summary presentation of his position more suitable for the lay reader is his *The Challenge of Jesus: Rediscovering Who Jesus Was and Is* (Downer's Grove, Ill.: InterVarsity Press, 1999) .

[5]For an extended list of authors who take this view, and for challenges to them, see the March/April 2000 issue of *Biblical Archeology,* vol. 26, no. 2,

specifically the articles "What Separates a Minimalist from a Maximalist? Not Much," by Philip Davies and "Save Us from Postmodern Malarkey," by William G. Dever.

[6]Wright, *The New Testament and the People of God*, 368. John Cobb describes what has happened as the "professionalization of theology" in *Reclaiming the Church* (Louisville: Westminster John Knox Press, 1997), 22–31.

―――― Chapter 1: What You Can Believe about the Bible ――――

[1]N. T. Wright points out that it is a faulty assumption to think that most early Christians were acquainted with or knew about the writings that we "casually pull off a shelf today and treat as 'typical' of first- or second-century Christianity" (*The New Testament and the People of God*, 359). Further, as Jewish Christians, what "scriptures" they did know about were initially those books Jews today call the Hebrew Bible, or what in the Christian Bible are called the Old Testament. The first known list of the books that later formed the New Testament was mentioned in a letter written by Athanasius, Bishop of Alexandria, dated 367 C.E. The Third Council of Carthage approved the same list in 397 C.E., and it was ratified by a papal decree in 405 C.E. A helpful resource for readers wanting to explore in detail issues related to the development of the Bible and its authority is Jeffrey L. Shelter, *Is the Bible True? How Modern Debates and Discoveries Affirm the Essence of the Scripture* (San Francisco: Harper SanFrancisco/Zondervan, 1999).

[2]There is also what might be called the *postmodern* view, which basically says that reality—knowledge included—is whatever I perceive it to be, that is, it is like the baseball umpire who neither calls 'em the way he sees 'em nor calls 'em the way they are, but declares, "They ain't nothing till I call 'em."

[3]Wright, *The New Testament and the People of God*, 64.

[4]Ibid., 124.

[5]Wright, *Jesus and the Victory of God*, 138.

[6]Wright, *The New Testament and the People of God*, 124.

[7]Wright argues that the gospel writers "believed themselves to be writing [what we call] history, the history of Jesus," precisely because they were convinced that he was the completion of Israel's history, real history in the real world (ibid., 397).

[8]Cobb, *Reclaiming the Church*, 46.

[9]Wright, *The New Testament and the People of God*, 140.

[10]Ibid., 141.

―――― Chapter 2: What You Can Believe about Jesus ――――

[1]The two primary creedal formulations are the Nicene Creed (325 C.E.) and the Apostles' Creed (sixth century C.E.).

[2]Annie Dillard, "The Gospel According to Saint Luke," in *Incarnation*, ed. Alfred Corn (New York: Penguin Books, 1990), 36.

[3]Karl Barth, *The Humanity of God* (Atlanta: John Knox Press, 1974).

[4]Wright, *The New Testament and the People of God*, 653.

[5]Ibid., 428–42.

[6]Ibid., 653.

[7]Wright, *Jesus and the Victory of God,* 615.

[8]Ibid., 653.

[9]Saint Augustine, *The City of God: An Abridged Version from the Translation by Gerald Walsh, Demetrius Zema, Grace Monahan, and Daniel Honan,* ed. Vernon J. Bourke (Garden City, N.Y.: Image Books, 1958), 278.

[10]For an extended discussion of these doctrines, Gustaf Aulen's *Christus Victor* (New York: Macmillan, 1931) remains a basic text.

[11]Nelson Mandela, *Long Walk to Freedom* (Boston: Little, Brown, Back Bay Books, 1994). The cover statement that the book "should be read by every person alive" is far from hyperbole.

[12]Wright, *The New Testament and the People of God,* 400.

[13]Luke Timothy Johnson, *Living Jesus: Learning the Heart of the Gospel* (San Francisco: HarperSanFrancisco, 1999), 6.

[14]Wright, *The Challenge of Jesus,* 127, in reference to the work of Barbara Thiering.

[15]The story of a British minister, A. W. Dale, as told by Leslie Weatherhead, *The Resurrection and the Life* (Nashville: Abingdon Press, 1968), 9.

[16]Ibid., 10.

[17]Pope John Paul II recently issued a statement that affirmed the Roman Catholic Church's position that heaven and hell are not places, but states of being.

[18]In *The Case for Christianity* (New York: Macmillan, Collier Books, 1989), C. S. Lewis described miracles in this way because, as he points out, the laws of nature that human beings take for granted "may not be anything except a way of speaking," and that when we speak of nature being governed by certain laws, all that means is "that nature does, in fact, behave in a certain way" (18). He also notes that the law of human nature, on the other hand, "tells us what humans should do but don't"(14–15).

[19]Nils Alstrup Dahl, *Jesus in the Memory of the Early Church* (Minneapolis: Augsburg, 1976). Specifically, "*To remember* in the New Testament signifies almost always to recall something or to think about it in such a way that it is expressed in speech or is formative for attitude and action." Further, "the Hebrew word zakar, 'to remember', carries the same meaning" (13).

[20]This is a direct quote from a lecture Jean Vanier gave in the fall of 2000 at Augsburg College, Minneapolis, Minn.

—— Chapter 3: What You Can Believe about God ——

[1]Lewis, *The Case for Christianity,* 5.

[2]Ibid.

[3]Figures from George Barna Associates, as reported on their Web site (www.barna.org) in the fall of 2000 prior to the release of *Rechurching the Unchurched* by George Barna, (Ventura, Calif.: Barna Associates, 2000), which contains a detailed report of this survey material based on a nationwide survey of 1,004 adults, ages eighteen and older, drawn randomly from the forty-eight continental states using a random-digit dial sampling technique. The data were collected via telephone interviews conducted during January 1996 as part of the

OmniPoll™ study by the Barna Research Group, Ltd., based in Glendale, California. It is estimated that the data are accurate to within plus or minus three percentage points of the total population response, based on a 95 percent confidence level.

[4]David Elton Trueblood, *Philosophy of Religion* (New York: Harper & Row, 1957), 270.

[5]Ibid., 273.

[6]For a balanced and in-depth study of this issue see Marianne Meye Thompson, *The Promise of the Father: Jesus and God in the New Testament* (Louisville: Westminster John Knox Press, 2000).

—— Chapter 4: What You Can Believe about the Holy Spirit ——

[1]Mandela, *Long Walk to Freedom,* 462.

—— Chapter 5: What You Can Believe about Moral Questions ——

[1]Michael Kinsley, "When reasonable people believe the unbeliever," *Minneapolis Star Tribune,* 31 December 2000, sec. A, 21.

[2]Dwight and Linda Vogel, *Sacramental Living: Falling Stars & Coloring Outside the Lines* (Nashville: Upper Room Books, 1999), 109–10.

[3]The study was sponsored by the Urban Institute, financed by the federal government, and provides the first national data on sexual practices of fifteen- to nineteen-year-old boys, as reported in the *Minneapolis Star Tribune,* 19 December 2000, sec. A, 15.

[4]Ibid.

[5]Maggie Gallagher, *The Abolition of Marriage: How We Destroy Lasting Love* (Washington, D.C.: Regnery Publications, 1996), 90. Gallagher, a syndicated conservative columnist, argues against no-fault divorce laws, which she claims have served to weaken the institution of marriage rather than serving as a way for people trapped in a bad situation to get out.

[6]Barna Associates, survey results from "Christians Are More Likely to Experience Divorce Than Are Non-Christians," December 21, 1999, as reported on the Barna Web site (www.barna.org).

[7]Richard Foster, *Sex, Money and Power: The Challenge of the Disciplined Life* (San Francisco: Harper & Row, 1985), 142–43.

[8]Larry Watson, *Laura* (New York: Penguin Books, 2000), 79–80.

[9]Peter J. Gomes, *The Good Book: Reading the Bible with Mind and Heart* (New York: Avon Books, 1996), 145. Open about his own homosexuality, Gomes calls the dominant attitude in the church toward homosexuals "The Last Prejudice" and presents a point of view that is solidly grounded in research without losing the personal dimension of this controversy.

[10]From an article entitled, "Presbyterians to vote on gays in pulpit," *Minneapolis Star Tribune,* 30 June 2001, Faith and Values section.

[11]Ibid.

[12]*Minneapolis Star Tribune,* 11 August 2000, sec. A, 19.

[13]Gomes, *The Good Book,* p. 146.

[14]A balanced discussion with in-depth articles presenting contrasting views can be found in Jeffrey L. Siker, *Homosexuality in the Church: Both Sides of the Debate* (Louisville: Westminster John Knox Press, 1994).

[15]John W. Gardner, *On Leadership* (New York: The Free Press, 1990), 101–2.

[16]Ibid., 102.

[17]Ibid.

[18]Ibid., 98.

[19]Ibid.

[20]Based on figures from the Alan Guttmacher Institute (AGI) and the Center for Disease Control (CDC) made available by the Robert Krawetz Web site, January 21, 2001.

[21]B. A. Robinson, "What the Bible Says About Abortion," an article published on the Web site for the Ontario Consultants on Religious Tolerance (www.religioustolerance.org).

[22]Ibid.

[23]Ralph Waldo Emerson, *Essays: First Series* (New York: Hurst & Company Publishers, n.d.), 33.

[24]"U.S. Bishops Statement on Capital Punishment" United States Catholic Conference, 1980, available from 3211 4th Street N. E., Washington, D.C. (www.nccbuscc.org).

[25]Tracy L. Snell, "Capital Punishment 1999," Bureau of Justice Statistics Bulletin, December 2000 (NCJ184795), U.S. Department of Justice (available as of January 2002 at www.usdoj.gov). Additional statistics on pages 105–6 from James Stephan and Peter Brien, "Capital Punishment 1993," Bureau of Justice Statistics Summary, December 1994 (NCJ 151786), U.S. Department of Justice (available as of January 2002 at www.usdoj.gov).

[26]*The Torah: A Modern Commentary* (New York: Union of American Hebrew Congregations, 1981), 907.

[27]Randy Furst, "Prisoner looks at freedom after 13 years on death row," *Minneapolis Star Tribune,* 1 January 2001, A1.

[28]Snell, "Capital Punishment 1999."

[29]Toni Locy, "Push to reform death penalty growing," *USA Today,* 20 February 2001, psec. 5A, 5.

[30]Snell, "Capital Punishment 1999."

[31]U.S. Bishop's statement, 1980.

[32]Robinson, *op. cit.,* "Religion and Prayer in U.S. Public Schools: Landmark Cases."Source for cases cited below: *Constitutional Law,* Horn Book Series, 5th ed.

[33]This version was altered numerous times as debate on it followed its public airing.

[34]The final version of the Istook bill that was approved by the House Judiciary Committee's Subcommittee on the Constitution October 28, 1997, read as follows: "To secure the people's right to acknowledge God according to the dictates of conscience: Neither the United States nor any State shall establish any official religion,

but the people's right to pray and to recognize their religious beliefs, heritage, or traditions on public property, including schools, shall not be infringed. Neither the United States nor any State shall require any person to join in prayer or other religious activity, prescribe school prayers, discriminate against religion, or deny equal access to a benefit on the account of religion." Source: religiousfreedom.house.gov.

[35]Thomas Jefferson on Politics and Government, "Letter From Danbury Baptist Association and Jefferson's Reply," University of Virginia Web site (etext.Virginia.edu). Jefferson's letter of 1802 was in response to one he received while President from The Danbury Baptist Association, concerned about religious liberty in the new nation, dated Oct. 7, 1801, and signed by Nehh Dodge, Ephram Robbins, and Stephen S. Nelson on behalf of the association. From *The Writings of Thomas Jefferson,* ed. Lipscomb and Bergh, memorial ed. (Washington, D.C.: Thomas Jefferson Memorial Assoc., 1903–04). Cited on the Eyler Robert Coates, Sr., Web site, "Thomas Jefferson On Politics & Government, Quotations from the writings of Thomas Jefferson," a Web site listed among links by the Jefferson Literary and Debating Society of the University of Virginia, http://scs.student.virginia.edu/~jefflds/jefferson.html.

[36]Ibid.

[37]Ibid.

[38]Alan M. Dershowitz, article written for the *Los Angeles Times,* published in the *Minneapolis Star Tribune,* 21 January 2001, editorial page.

[39]Central Conference of American Rabbis, "Resolution on Religion in Public EducationSchools," 95th Convention of the Central Conference of American Rabbis meeting in Grossingers, N.Y., June 18–21, 1984 (www.ccarnet.org).

[40]Union of American Hebrew Congregations (UAHC), "Resolution on Religion in Public Education," 46th Assembly of the Union of American Hebrew Congregations (UAHC), 1961, meeting in Washington, D.C. (www.uahc.org).

—— Chapter 6: What You Can Believe about Other Religions ——

[1]In 2000 Ihsan Bagby of Shaw University in Raleigh, North Carolina, led a project cosponsored by the Islamic Society of North America that included interviews with 416 leaders of the roughly 1,200 mosques currently in the United States. The interviews revealed that there are approximately 6 to 7 million Americans who consider themselves orthodox Moslems and that 77 percent of the mosques reported significant numerical growth in attendance. Cited in Ken Kusner, "Scholars study role of mosques," *Minneapolis Star Tribune,* 21 July 2001, sec. B, 7.

[2]Reported in Dave Smith, "Planned visit by Dalai Lama miffs legislator," *Minneapolis Star Tribune,* 8 May 2001, sec. B, 5.